HOW to GET to The PALACE From YOUR PRISON!

Joseph's 14-Step Program to Overcome Loneliness, Depression, Discrimination, Barrenness, & Abuse

C. Joyce Farrar-Rosemon

ISBN 0985626224
ISBN 978-0-9856262-2-8

Printed in the United States of America

WINNER AT LIFE PUBLISHERS
ATLANTA, GEORGIA 30281
WWW.WOMENSEMPOWERMENTSEMINARS.COM
404-202-8776

IN MEMORIAM

To Tiffany, my stillborn daughter:
Your death brought a resurrection and a desire
to seek that place of Shalom in my spirit.
Thank you for being a ministering angel in my life.
(Hebrews 1:13-14)

CONTENTS

ACKNOWLEDGEMENTS

To my beloved son, David, and my cherished husband, Tillmon: Thank you both for teaching me daily how to practice forgiveness and give unconditional love.

To my spiritual family, Word of Faith Family Cathedral of Atlanta, Georgia: Thank you God for the synergy that flows from this church body; the ushers, the singers, the pastors and the efficacious words and songs of Bishop Dale C. Bronner and his lovely wife, Dr. Nina Bronner, which allow us to usher in the presence of God in our lives.

INTRODUCTION

Many have heard the story found in Genesis of how Joseph, hated by his brothers, and thrown in prison later became the head of Egypt. We marvel at Joseph's faith and tenacity, but do we understand that his rags-to-riches story has been left as a blueprint for us to rise above our present-day circumstances and become *the head* in all our endeavors in life. The story of Joseph is a road map as to how we can excel in our relationships, health, finances, and spiritual life. It details how we can leave a financial, but of more importance, a spiritual legacy for our children's children.

In the following chapters, I will lay out how Joseph took 14 steps towards his spiritual and emotional maturity. I will detail how he washed his ornamented robe, and got a new one that could not be stripped by his brothers or fellow man. I will show how we too can take these 14 steps, and get to the palace from our prison, and be the head of our emotions, health, finances, thoughts, spiritual life and relationships.

This writing is a sequel to my book, *HOW to BE the HEAD and NOT the TAIL! A Christian Manifesto for Making Six Figures* (Providence House Publishers). In *HOW to BE the HEAD and NOT the TAIL!* I delineate the biblical and business principles as to how one can discover their true calling in life, and make six figures or more.

In this writing, I show the reader in depth the steps to take to overcome the obstacles that prevent us from getting to our preordained destiny. I serve as a spiritual coach, a mentor to walk the reader through the dark tunnels of life. Let this book you are holding in your hands be a tangible reminder that as Jesus was the fourth man, and walked with me and many others through our fiery furnaces of afflictions to that place of "shalom," he will do the same for anyone who calls on his name. The Hebrew word for peace is "shalom," which means "nothing missing and nothing broken."

The world that we live in today has become increasingly unstable, unsafe, and a violent place to live in. Advances in science, medicine and technology are failing to bring about peace and security in the world. Western society appears to be coming apart at the seams as we allocate more money for prisons, national defense, and space exploration. Statistics on depression, suicide, unemployment, discrimination, and domestic and child abuse are alarming, and point to a menacing cancer that is eating away at the fabric of our families, and Western society. The canary sent into the mine of our society is dying by the minute. The handwriting is not only on the walls of our homes, but also its fulfilled prophecy - the bodies of unloved sons and daughters lie dead beneath the graffiti on our streets.

Where is the physician that will resurrect individuals that have let their dreams, prophecies, and aspirations die? Where is the physician that will rise and be healed, and heal others? Where is the physician that will heal the walking wounded that are still alive and have a small measure of hope?

How to GET to the PALACE from YOUR PRISON reveals how Joseph was inspired by the Great Physician, achieved the promises of God, and arrived at that place of shalom in his mind, body, and spirit. The Bible tells us that there is nothing new under the sun. God is the same yesterday, today, and forever more. The Bible is not only a historical document, but it is also an allegory containing spiritual truths and laws. Accordingly, these truths that allowed past believers to be more than conquerors through Christ are still able to empower modern day believers to conquer enemies and achieve victory.

This 14-Step Recovery program will provide the footprints in the sands of life for you to follow, so that you can walk through the valley of the shadow of death and fear no evil. It will serve as a compass so that you can experience shalom wherever you find yourself today: in a prison [mental, emotional, or physical] or a palace, unemployed or financially independent, in sickness or in health. It will detail how to store up grain spiritually, so that regardless of the economy or your state of mind, you and your descendants will be able to overcome any famine that you may face in your journey through life. And lastly, this 14-Step

Program will show you how to leave a warranty deed for your genetic and spiritual descendants, so that generational curses are broken. It is designed to empower your descendants to become the *head* and not the *tail,* and most important of all arrive at their *palace*, their place of shalom.

To the reader, my prayer is that you will become like the mighty palm tree. May your spiritual roots become grounded so that when the hurricanes of life come, you will be able to bend as the storm passes over you. And then, like the palm tree, erect yourself afterwards so that you can stand, prosper, and get to the palace, that place of shalom in your mind, body and spirit.

Step 1
Discovering Your Gifts

Joseph had a dream, and when he told it to his brothers, they hated him all the more.

Genesis 37:5 NIV

Joseph realized at the young age of 17 that God spoke to him through dreams, and that he had a special anointing from God to interpret them. Joseph's brothers hated him because of his blessings from God, and also that their father favored Joseph above them. Their hatred and jealousy was so intense that they ostracized him, and would not commune with their baby brother in a loving manner. The ornamented robe, and Joseph sharing of his dreams of reigning over them further alienated him from his brothers. Their anger climaxed in their attempt to kill him, and supposedly his dreams.

The ornamented robe Joseph's father gave him is a metaphor for the love, the favor, and the attention their father showered on Joseph. His clothing symbolized the gifts and the talents God had given to Joseph. This robe is also a symbol of our lives- how we carry ourselves, how we conduct ourselves. It is a metaphor for what's inside of us. God is no respecter of persons. He has given everyone a robe in the form of talents and abilities.

Throughout the Bible, God is trying to convey to us an understanding of these truths. In the New Testament Jesus shared this message with us in the Parable of the Talents. The challenge in life is how to best use our natural talents and abilities. We must ask ourselves, - are we wasting our one talent and hiding it, simply because we think that God is austere and unfair to us, as in this parable? Or have we fallen into the trap of comparing our one gift, our robe with what others are adorned with and saying ours is not enough? I'm curious as to why we don't use what we have and trust that God will supply our remaining needs.

The Word says that the Earth is the Lord's, and the fullness thereof. The second premise is that God's will is that we have life, and that more abundantly. In spite of these two Biblical truths, many still take the path of least resistance and choose to complain, instead of calling forth in word and deed the dreams and desires of our heart. The Bible postulates two questions for our perusal. The first is, why are we sitting waiting to die rather than going after the good of the land (II Kings 7:3-4)? And secondly, why do we sit like the man by the pool of Bethesda for 38 years (John 5:2-9) waiting for someone to put us in the pool and make us whole?

I wonder why as we grow older we lose the fearlessness that a child displays that would motivate us to take the first step towards the pool. We start off life full of joy and enthusiasm, and then we end up sitting around for 38 years of our life, complaining rather than applying action to our desires and taking that first small step. We procrastinate or avoid signing up for that course of higher learning that will take us to the next level, or we won't consistently set aside a small amount of funds so that we can buy our first home or investment property. Many of us will allow ourselves to remain in abusive relationships that diminish our self-esteem. Others can give you a speech on the benefits of exercise, eating the right foods, but won't move away from the table when they have had enough. What is the self-hatred that causes us to do wrong, when we know we should do right?

In the face of abundance, why do we allow others to tell us that we have nothing to draw from (John 4:11)? The Word says that of his fullness, all we have received (John 1:16). All that we need to sustain life is in us prior to conception. It further states that before we were formed in our mother's belly, God knew us and preordained for us to be the *head* and not the *tail* from the very beginning.

Our job is to obey God's Word, and draw from his everlasting water so that we have no need to thirst anymore (John 4:14). Once we do that, then not only is our life full in the natural, but more importantly, we will inherit eternal life with the Father, where there will be no crying or dying. Only peace, thanksgiving, joy, tranquility, and hope eternal will reign in our lives. Nothing missing, nothing broken- this is *shalom*.

Any gift from God will be tested to see if the recipient is worthy of it. To one whom much is given, much is required. Joseph had to learn like Job that there is a cost associated with blessings from God, and the receiver must be willing to make sacrifices for these blessings. The sacrifice will cost you something dear- for Abraham, it was the possible loss of his son Isaac, or a worse scenario, being beheaded like John the Baptist. Dr. Martin Luther King gave his life for not just blacks, but for all of mankind wherever oppression existed on this planet. Countless Africans, descendants of Africans, and slaves lost their lives because of their robes of blackness. Many Jews, Christians, and Muslims have also lost their lives for their religious robes. We must all answer the question of what we are willing to die for. It is said that we really don't start living until we find something to die for.

In II Kings 7:3-8, four lepers could not go in and enjoy the good of the land because of their robes of leprosy. Their leprosy tarnished their self-image. They perceived themselves as being unworthy, and therefore not entitled to enjoy the fruits of the land. Because of their false perception, they did not realize that they already possessed the land. In their ignorance of their true self-image, they did not realize that they had the title deed in their hands that would enable them to possess the land.

By obeying God, [following the steps in the title deed, which is the Word of God] they received a new robe in the form of new clothes, silver, gold and choice foods. In the face of impending death, one of them mustered up enough courage and stepped out on faith and decided that it was better to die trying to overcome the famine in the land than to do nothing and die anyway. Clearly, what the enemy meant for evil, God turned it around and made it good because of one man's faith.

What are you doing with your "robe," the gifts that God has given to you? Are you comparing it to someone else's and saying that your robe is not favorably adorned. God loves you, and He gave you His very best when He gave his Son, so that we might have life in abundance here on Earth, and live eternally with Him in heaven. The Bible tells us to count it all as joy when we suffer for the gospel, knowing that our reward will be great

(James 1:2-12). This should be our quest: to be numbered with those who have washed "their robes" in the blood of the Lamb (Rev. 7:14).

How do we as modern-day Christians wash our robes and cleanse ourselves from our skin conditions that cause us to question whether we are the right gender, physical shape, race, color, or nationality? Issues of rejection concerning our exterior appearance can also be based on a speech impediment, a physical, emotional, or mental disability. Or alternatively, how do we handle the discrimination that we may encounter just because someone perceives that what we have is somehow better than what they have? What effective approaches are available to handle the rejection that is based on our exterior appearance, *the robe* that God has given us?

One option is to follow the approach that Joseph used by obeying the Word of God. I want to underscore that this washing, this cleansing of Joseph's robe, i.e., his obeying of the Word of God, was what made him successful. At the core of Joseph's being, he trusted that his dreams [his gifts] were valid, and he made a decision to endure until they materialized. Joseph's dreams eventually manifested and he became the head of the Egyptian government.

He also got a new robe- an Egyptian one symbolizing his mastery of the world. But of more importance, he received a new robe of righteousness, because he had endured the fight of faith. Once you get your robe of righteousness, then it is just a matter of time before you see the outward manifestation of headship in all your endeavors. You can also rise above the effects of poverty, disease, discrimination, depression, a single parent home, and other ills, and become a Harriet Tubman, a President Lincoln, a Madame C. J. Walker, a Helen Keller, a Mother Teresa, a President Clinton, a President Mandela or a President Obama.

Step 2
Understanding Your Dreams and Visions

Then he [Joseph] remembered his dreams…

Genesis 42:9 NIV

Regardless of where life took Joseph, he never let go of his understanding of what God had placed in his heart. Joseph accepted the anointing on his life to hear from God through dreams, and to interpret them. This gift was like a visual manifestation of speaking in tongues (Act 2:4) and interpreting them. Joseph did not question his anointing, or doubt his dreams simply because they were not politically correct, or that they caused him to be sold into slavery for thirteen years, and then imprisoned for over two years.

Speaking in "tongues" is outward communication with God. They are messages coming from the spirit man. Dreams that come from God represent a form of inward communication with him. In "visions of the night," God speaks to us. (Job 4:13, 33:14-18). It is then that He can get our attention. Dreams can be informative, prophetic or revelatory. God uses dreams to guide, build a hedge around us, and protect us from our enemies and future unseen harm.

In Genesis 20, Abimelech averted a premature death because he followed the instructions in a dream. In Genesis 28, God revealed to Jacob in a dream that the Abrahamic covenant for all of mankind would be established in spite of Jacob's deceptive spirit and imperfections. In Genesis 31, Jacob confessed that a prosperity plan revealed to him in a dream when he was being taken advantage of by his father-in law, Laban, had caused him to gain the flock of Laban [the wealth of his adversary]. Although Laban and his sons were incensed that Jacob had gained all their wealth, they could not touch Jacob or his transferred wealth from them. God had put a hedge of protection around Jacob by speaking to Laban in a dream and commanding him not to harm Jacob.

God reveals the secret things to those that are his chosen ones, those that are willing to seek Him and go apart to the secret place of the most high (Isaiah 45:3, Psalm 91:1). In Genesis 41, God used a dream to trouble the Pharaoh, a heathen, but its interpretation and the destiny of nations lay in the hands of Joseph, a prisoner. None of the Pharaoh's wise men and magicians throughout the land of Egypt could interpret the Pharaoh's dreams. With all their education and training, they were all clueless as to their meaning. Only Joseph was given the ability to save nations from famine because of his God-given gift to interpret dreams.

Madame C. J. Walker, who grew up in poverty, unable to read or write, became America's first black millionaire. The book, *African American Women Scientists and Inventors*, by Otha Richard Sullivan, states that Ms. Walker's million dollar invention came to her in a dream during a time she had faced so many catastrophes that her hair began to fall out. "One night, I had a dream," she recounted. "A man appeared to me and told me what to mix up for my hair. Some of the remedy was grown in Africa, but I sent for it, put it on my scalp, and in a few weeks, my hair was coming in faster than it had ever fallen out." [1]

World-renowned Helen Keller also had a dream after she was struck with an illness that left her blind, deaf, and unable to communicate at 5 months shy of her second birthday. Modern doctors and researchers are not sure whether it was meningitis, scarlet fever, or a severe bout of encephalitis.

Helen's favorite childhood dream of attending college was one she later achieved. In 1900 Helen reached her goal and attended Radcliff College. By the time Helen was 24 she had graduated college with a Bachelor of Arts degree. She was the first deaf blind woman to receive this degree. Later on Radcliff dedicated a garden in her name and gave her the Alumnae Achievement Award.

Helen Keller spent her adult life drawing awareness to the blind and deaf community. She traveled to 30 different countries

[1] Sullivan,Otha Richard. *African American Women Scientists and Inventors.* (New York: Wiley, 2002), 27.

to demonstrate that blind and deaf people could still function in society. She became one of the world's leading women. The last public appearance she made was in 1961 at a Lion's meeting. She was presented with an award for her service to humanity over her life.

Helen Keller received many awards during the course of her life. Among them the Presidential Medal of Freedom, Brazil's Order of the Southern Cross, the Philippines' Golden Heart, Japan's Sacred Treasure, and in 1991, was named one of the most important people of the twentieth century by Life magazine. She was affectionately given the title of "the first lady of courage."

In the following poem written by Helen Keller, she eloquently described how God transformed her favorite childhood dream into a reality:

They took away what should have been my eyes
(But I remembered Milton's Paradise).
They took away what should have been my ears,
(Beethoven came and wiped away my tears).
They took away what should have been my tongue,
(But I had talked with God when I was young).
He would not let them take away my soul –
Possessing that, I still possess the whole. [2]

I would be shamefully remiss to talk about the power and purpose of dreams and not mention Reverend Dr. Martin Luther King's world acclaimed, "I Have a Dream" speech delivered under the auspices of the Lincoln Memorial. His dream ushered us into God's courtroom of justice and equality. And his sacrificial death not only opened the freedom doors for people of color, it also opened doors for women, poor whites, and others world-wide who found themselves in oppressive and unjust situations.

Facing constant death threats, he proclaimed prophetically on the eve of his assassination in his "I See the Promised Land" speech, the following:

---

[2] http://www.hyperhistory.net/apwh/bios/b4hkeller_p1cg.htm

> Well, I don't know what will happen now. We've got some difficult days ahead. But it doesn't matter with me now. Because I've been to the mountaintop. And I don't mind. Like anybody, I would like to live a long life. Longevity has its place. But I'm not concerned about that now. I just want to do God's will. And He's allowed me to go up to the mountain. And I've looked over. And I've seen the promised land. I may not get there with you. But I want you to know tonight, that we, as a people will get to the promised land. And I'm happy, tonight. I'm not worried about anything. I'm not fearing any man. Mine eyes have seen the glory of the coming of the Lord.[3]

Learn not to despise your secret place, though it may appear to imprison you. Although you may feel alone and wonder why others are not willing to burn the midnight oil - they don't want to go to church or read, and apply the teachings of the Bible - don't despise your small beginnings. Know that your prison, your hardship serves a purpose. What the enemy meant for evil, God can and will turn around and establish His plan for your life, and for mankind as well.

Jacob described his dilemma, his suffering and redemption as follows in Genesis 31:40-42 NIV:

> ...The heat consumed me in the daytime and the cold at night, and sleep fled from my eyes. It was like this for the twenty years I was in your household. I worked for you fourteen years for your two daughters and six years for your flocks, and you changed my wages ten times. If the God of my father, the God of Abraham and the fear of Isaac, had not been with me, you would surely have sent me away empty-handed. But God has seen my hardship and the toil of my hands, and last night he rebuked you.

Take comfort in these words from Jacob, and know that your

---

[3] Washington, James M., ed., *A Testament Of Hope: The Essential Writings And Speeches Of Martin Luther King, Jr.* (New York: Harper Collins, 1991), 286.

suffering is also redemptive, and that your suffering is only for a season. Know and understand that you are not being ostracized and set apart for vindictive purposes. You are never alone, because greater is He that is within you than he that is in the world (I John 4:4). Know that your suffering, if you stick to God's plan and obey his Word, will bring about a harvest in your life, and in the lives of generations to follow.

God's promise is to be there with you when you go through the valley of the shadow of death. To comfort, keep, restore, and vindicate you. God's promise is to rebuke the enemy when He sees that you are covered with the blood of Jesus.

The Bible gives us many instructions on how to handle a troubled heart in times of distress and despair. In John 14:1-3, we are told:

> Let not your heart be troubled: ye believe in God, believe also in me. In my Father's house are many mansions: if it were not so, I would have told you. I go to prepare a place for you. And if I go and prepare a place for you, I will come again, and receive you unto myself; that where I am, there ye may be also. Proverbs 4:23 tells us to, Keep thy heart with all diligence; for out it are the issues of life.

In Matthew 5:8, we are instructed that if we want to see God, then we must have a pure heart. It is not enough just to have a dream or a vision for your future. You must also have a pure heart, like Joseph. God prepared a mansion for Joseph, and He has also prepared physical, but more importantly, ethereal mansions [including expansive levels of consciousness, higher thinking, wisdom, and understanding] for all of us. But if our heart is troubled, we can't get to the palace, that place of shalom. Joseph's heart was pure, whether he was abased or esteemed. He saw God as ordering his footsteps and preparing a way in the wilderness of his life experiences.

When your heart is pure, you know who you are, like Joseph did. Your self-esteem is intact. As the seed of Abraham, you are anointed and empowered to go through the valley of the shadow of death. During times of adversity, you don't lose confidence. Like Chris Gardner's son in the movie, *The Pursuit of*

Happyness, you are able to say to our heavenly Father, "I trust you," even if you are homeless, bedridden, in prison, or emotionally distressed.

Not only was Joseph's heart pure, but he also knew the Word. When you know the Word and you stand on it with a pure heart, you can do miracles. You can walk on water, take two small fish and five loaves of bread and feed thousands, turn water into wine [mourning into gladness], defeat the enemies within and without, and turn what the enemy meant for evil into something good.

Like a photograph, it is in these dark places that we are processed and developed. Know that when God has tried you through the fire, and established His Word in you, that you shall come forth as pure gold. You shall be the *head* and not the *tail*! Know that it is only in the secret place that God can reveal His Word to you. You must learn to separate yourself from the modern day magicians and wise men. You must learn to close your ears to the negative news reports, media, statistics, and predictors of doom and gloom.

You must saturate yourself with God's gospel; his good news that says the Earth is the Lord's and the fullness thereof. He came that we might have life and it more abundantly. As you seek, you will find, as you knock, doors will be opened unto you. No good thing will God deny to those that love Him. You have already been given the title deed - the houses, and the palaces. They are yours by divine inheritance, but you must use the key, which is obedience to the Word of God, to unlock the door.

In summary, God uses dreams to give us victory over death, disease, famine, abuse, poverty, mistreatment, injustices, the unknown, and the future. They are given to heathens and believers alike, to establish God's purpose here on Earth. They can be used as well to bring heathens to an acceptance of God's power.

Write down your dreams and keep them in a journal. Ask God to reveal to you what they mean. Joseph acknowledged that it was not in his power to interpret dreams. He told the Pharaoh, "I cannot do it." Joseph made it plain that it was God's doing. At the risk of being sent back to prison, Joseph did not try to take the credit to save his own hide. How many of us facing a return to years of imprisonment [mentally, emotionally, or physically] or even death would acknowledge that it is God that has given us our special talents and abilities?

Although Joseph desperately wanted to get out of prison (Genesis 40:14-15), he made himself vulnerable to prolonging that experience by being honest and not taking credit for his gift. He was not like his great-grandfather, the untransformed Abram, who denied that Sarai was his wife in order to avoid possible death (Genesis 12:11-16).

As you see, the manifestations of your dreams and gifts come into reality, follow Joseph's example and give God the glory. Make it plain that this gift is God's doing and that God is not a respecter of persons. Let others know that if we as believers are willing to go within to our secret place, God will reveal to us plans for success, prosperity, inventions, creative ideas, etc. Share freely and openly with others that God's will for them is that they have an abundant life, full of joy and peace.

Step 3
Defeating Dysfunctional Behavior

Now Israel [Jacob] loved Joseph more than any of his other sons, because he had been born to him of his old age; and he made a richly ornamented robe for him.

Genesis 37:3 NIV

There are many reasons why Joseph was a special, highly favored child. The fact that he was born to Jacob in his old age was only one of them. Jacob had labored for seven years for Joseph's mother, Rachel, after being tricked and deceived into marrying Rachel's sister, Leah. Jacob and Rachel also suffered years of barrenness before Joseph was born. Eleven children were born to Jacob through his other three wives before Rachel gave birth to their treasured child. Joseph, named by his mother, means, "may He add." Joseph was indeed a special, long awaited for child that was finally added to their family.

It is easy to understand why Joseph was so cherished and highly favored. Joseph was the consummation of years of prayer, longing, suffering, tears and anguish. Joseph was the embodiment of Rachel's prophetic prayer that God would add to her the desire of her heart, which was to have additional offspring. Unfortunately, she did not live to see that through Joseph her seed added greatly to the kingdom of God, and continues to be a blessing to all nations to this day.

Barrenness or infertility can be very painful, especially when you are blessed and have prospered in other areas of your life, but can't consummate your love by producing fruit from that marriage in the form of a child. Barrenness, in some cases can lead to divorce, or cause one to do irrational things, like abduct a baby from a hospital, or commit an unconscionable act of killing a mother in order to steal her baby. Having personally endured two miscarriages, a stillbirth, and barrenness myself, I understand all too well the taunting, the longing, the desperation, and grief Hannah felt in I Samuel 1: 1-16. As Hannah was blessed with a special child – Rachel, Jacob, my husband and I were eventually blessed with special children as well.

Of significance in our society are two diametrically opposed phenomena that have escalated over the past thirty years in the United States. Since 1973, over 48 million abortions have been performed since the U.S. Supreme Court legalized unrestricted abortion, according to the National Right to Life Organization.[4] Concurrently, infertility - the inability of a couple to conceive a pregnancy after trying to do so for at least one full year - has increased over the last 30 years.[5] According to Hopexchange, of the 4.4 million confirmed pregnancies every year, approximately 26,000 end in a stillbirth and approximately 500,000 end in miscarriage.[6]

Ironically, many of the same stress factors- the environment, pollution, age, health status, occupational exposure to solvents or toxins, or income problems can determine whether a pregnancy comes to term or not, and survives. An embryo has no choice as to which parents conceive and carry it to full-term. As a therapist, the pain, the hurt, and the trauma are evident, and felt by all individuals involved. The miracle of life, cut short for whatever reason, is not easily accepted or forgotten.

Marriage and children can also become incongruous for some parents. The responsibility of marriage and rearing children can cause one to miss the carefree days of youth and self-indulgence. There are other forms of barrenness that are just as painful. A divorcee, widow(er), or single person can experience barrenness in the form of loneliness that develops from a lack of companionship. Death, a chemical imbalance or addiction, a physical disability, unemployment, underemployment, and the inability to birth or sustain a business can create a sense of barrenness as well.

University of Western Ontario researcher, William Avison, Ph.D., looked at the link between losing a job and emotional problems. His study of almost 900 Canadian families found

---

[4] http://www.nrlc.org/abortion/facts/abortionstats.html

[5] http://www.healthline.com/galecontent/infertility-2

[6] http://www.hopexchange.com/Statistics.htm

strikingly high levels of psychological problems among the unemployed - 55 to 75 percent greater than in those who were working steadily. Complaints ranged from depression and substance abuse to panic attacks and anxiety. The study also found that wives of unemployed men experience dramatic mental health difficulties.[7]

Current discrimination statistics paint a troubling picture of the frequency and severity of employee lawsuits, and point to a general barrenness felt by many employees. Disgruntled workers typically allege discrimination based on sex, disability, age, race or religion; wrongful termination; invasion of privacy; and wrongful demotion or failure to promote. Employment liability claims have risen 400 percent in the past two decades, to the point that an average of 6.5 claims per 1,000 employees is brought annually. In fact, in a survey conducted by the Society for Human Resource Management (SHRM), more than 60 percent of all U. S. companies are sued by employees, or former employees annually.[8]

Success can also bring about a sense of barrenness, and does not come without a price tag. Success can cause one to experience a sense of loneliness for the friends, family members, and business associates that are not promoted to the next level with you. And of course, serious illnesses, "incurable" diseases, or being in a tumultuous relationship or marriage can create a sense of barrenness, a longing for peace in one's life.

In times of barrenness, wrestling with God and seeking Him has a way of bringing forth a search for that Lost Coin that is within us all (Luke 15:8-10). A state of barrenness, when you are totally helpless to perform a thing, and you seek God diligently, gives Him an opportunity to show off and do the miraculous. It gives God the opportunity to demonstrate that He does love us, and that He will fulfill His promise to give us more than we can ever imagine (I Cor 2:9).

When Joseph told his father about his dream of headship, Jacob "kept the matter in mind." As Mary had pondered about

---

[7] http://psychologytoday.com/articles/pto-19960901-000021.html

[8] http://compli.com/pdf/Employee_Relations_Law.pdf

the Christ child, Jacob had enough spiritual sense not to disregard Joseph's dream. Even though from all appearances it seemed there was no way that Joseph could become a ruler, Jacob did not challenge his son. As Jacob aged, he obviously had learned some important lessons about relationships, people, his walk with God, and Joseph. Jacob protected Joseph, and kept Joseph close to him, and did not send him with his brothers to graze their flocks. I'm sure that during these times, they had many long conversations about life, God, and what Joseph meant to his parents and to the seed of Abraham.

Jacob, too, was born to older parents. His father, Isaac, was sixty years old at the time of Jacob's birth. God also favored Jacob. Like Joseph, Jacob also had a dream in which God revealed to him, in Genesis 28, that Jacob would be the *head* and not the *tail*. Joseph, like his father was determined, willing to work hard, and was a good businessman.

Joseph was a manifestation of the refined and reformed Jacob that had become Israel. The generational curse of a deceitful spirit was not passed on to Joseph. The sins of the old Jacob - deceit, jealousy, envy - were passed on to the ten sons of his youth, but the sons of the new Jacob - Joseph and Benjamin - received the blessings of the new Jacob (Israel) who had struggled with God and men, and had prevailed (Gen. 32:25-28).

Isaac had seen obedience demonstrated through his father, Abraham, who presented Isaac as a sacrifice to God. Jacob had obviously learned obedience from Isaac, who did not resist his father's (Abraham) offering of him as a living sacrifice. Joseph practiced obedience at home, in Potiphar's house and in prison. The transformed Jacob (Israel) had obviously taught Joseph the Word.

Wherever Joseph went, he demonstrated obedience to God's Word. Although his brothers hated Joseph and would not speak a kind word to him, Joseph obeyed his father and went looking for them. In Potiphar's house, though he was well built and handsome, Joseph refused repeated sexual advances from Potiphar's wife. In prison, Joseph worked diligently and was put in charge of all those who were held there. Obedience brought success and prosperity to his master, and all that his master owned.

Through obedience to God's Word, Joseph mastered living in a hostile, quarrelsome, dysfunctional family and environment. Obedience to God's word is the key to success - though painful, unfair, and lonely at times; it does bring about an exceedingly good harvest. Mark 10:29-30 explains this principle as follows:

> ...There is no man that hath left house, or brethen, or sisters, or father, or mother, or wife, or children, or lands, for my sake, and the gospel's, But he shall receive an hundred-fold now in this time, houses and brethen, and sisters, and mothers, and children, and lands, *with persecutions*; and in the world to come eternal life.

Clearly, Joseph received more than a hundredfold return on the seeds he had sown of obedience, kindness, love, and forgiveness. Not only did Joseph master the fruits of the spirit found in Galatians 5:22-23; love, joy, peace, patience, kindness, goodness, faithfulness, gentleness and self-control, but he also mastered the secular world as well. Joseph mastered the Egyptian language, culture, and their methods of commerce and trade. He was such an astute businessman that the Pharaoh wanted to promote anyone else in his family that had special abilities. It was no wonder that Joseph was put in charge of all of Egypt. The blessings of Abraham were indeed upon Joseph. It was clear to believers and heathens alike that this was God's doings, and that the Lord had given Joseph success in whatever he did.

God is not a respecter of persons. Do not despise your beginnings if you feel that you are in a barren place and have not been given a coat of many colors like Joseph. God's Word says that by faith, we too are of the seed of Abraham, and consequently, we are entitled to be the *head* and not the *tail*. As the Lord blessed Joseph, He wants to bless us in the same measure. The key to Joseph's success and ours is so simple that we usually miss it. It is the blessing of obedience found in Deuteronomy 28:1-14 NIV:

> If you fully obey the LORD your God and carefully follow all

his commands I give you today, the LORD your God will set you high above all the nations on earth. All these blessings will come upon you and accompany you if you obey the LORD your God: You will be blessed in the city and blessed in the country. The fruit of your womb will be blessed, and the crops of your land and the young of your livestock—the calves of your herds and the lambs of your flocks. Your basket and your kneading trough will be blessed. You will be blessed when you come in and blessed when you go out. The LORD will grant that the enemies who rise up against you will be defeated before you. They will come at you from one direction but flee from you in seven. The LORD will send a blessing on your barns and on everything you put your hand to. The LORD your God will bless you in the land he is giving you. The LORD will establish you as his holy people, as he promised you on oath, *if you keep the commands of the LORD your God and walk in his ways*. Then all the peoples on earth will see that you are called by the name of the LORD, and they will fear you. The LORD will grant you abundant prosperity—in the fruit of your womb, the young of your livestock and the crops of your ground—in the land he swore to your forefathers to give you. The LORD will open the heavens, the storehouse of his bounty, to send rain on your land in season and to bless all the work of your hands. You will lend to many nations but will borrow from none. *The LORD will make you the head, not the tail.* If you pay attention to the commands of the LORD your God that I give you this day and carefully follow them, you will always be at the top, never at the bottom. Do not turn aside from any of the commands I give you today, to the right or to the left, *following other gods and serving them.*

In support of women, I think it is important to address the concerns of women in relation to obedience and submission in our male dominated, chauvinistic society. As some misguided individuals have erroneously used the Bible to support the horrific and inhumane enslavement of Africans and African Americans, in a similar fashion it has also been used too many times to keep women in a position of bondage, of second-class citizenship. There are many women who outwardly have an appearance of fulfillment in their marriage, but inwardly there is a sense of barrenness, a sense of unfulfillment in their life-spiritually, mentally, emotionally, and personally.

The scripture "Wives, submit yourselves unto your own husbands, as unto the Lord." (Ephesians 5:22) has been used time and time again to keep married women in a state of bondage and submission to their husbands. "Let your women keep silence in the churches... and if they learn anything, let them ask their husbands at home," (I Cor 14:34-35) is another scripture that is used to keep women in general - single, divorced or married - *in a state of submission to men.*

We then wonder why the divorce rate among Christian couples is so high, and why women are turning to other women as lovers. Many lesbians have actually been hurt, abused or mistreated by men [and sometimes women] in their lives, and now maintain a wall of defense by embracing lesbianism. Statistics concerning the mistreatment and abuse of women and children, as well as the disintegration of the Western family are frightening:

> **Domestic Abuse**
> Estimates range from 960,000 incidents of violence against a current or former spouse, boyfriend, or girlfriend per year, to three million women who are physically abused by their husband or boyfriend per year. Around the world, at least one in every three women has been beaten, coerced into sex ,or otherwise abused during her lifetime. Nearly one-third of American women (31 percent) report being physically or sexually abused by a husband or boyfriend at some point in their lives, according to a 1998 Commonwealth Fund survey. Women are seven to 14 times more likely than men to report suffering severe physical assaults from an intimate partner. The health-related costs of rape, physical assault, stalking, and homicide by intimate partners exceed five point eight billion dollars each year (CDC study). On average, more than three women are murdered by their husbands or boyfriends in this country every day. In 2000, 1,247 women were killed by an intimate partner. The same year, 440 men were killed by an intimate partner.[9]

---

[9] http://www.endabuse.org/resources/facts/DomesticViolence.pdf

Divorce

Divorce is on the decline, according to an USA TODAY article by Sharon Jayson. But it is suggested that this is due more to an increase in people living together than to more lasting marriages. According to The State of our Unions 2005 report, the U.S. divorce rate is 17.7 per 1,000 married women, down from 22.6 in 1980. The marriage rate is also on a steady decline: a 50% drop since 1970 from 76.5 per 1,000 unmarried women to 39.9, says the report, whose calculations are based on an internationally used measurement. Cohabiting couples have twice the breakup rate of married couples according to David Popence, co-author. In the U.S. 40% of these couples bring kids into these often-shaky live-in relationships, which results in the U.S. having the weakest families in the Western world. According to Popence, this is because we have the highest divorce rate and the highest rate of solo parenting. [10]

Christian Divorce

Stacy Hamby in her article, *Why can't Christians stay married*? researched this subject and found that divorce is more prevalent among Christians than the rest of the population. Ms. Hamby cited recent studies by the Barna Research Group that revealed that 27 percent of born-again Christians have been divorced. That compares with 24 percent of adults who are not born-again. According to federal census numbers, the so-called Bible Belt states have the highest divorce rates in the nation. Except for Nevada, where fast divorces are traditionally easy to get, Arkansas, Alabama, Oklahoma and Tennessee lead the nation in divorces. [11]

Domestic Violence and Children

In a national survey of more than 6,000 American families, 50 percent of the men who frequently assaulted their wives also frequently abused their children.[12] Studies suggest that between three point three and ten million children witness some form of domestic violence annually.[13]

---

[10] http://www.usatoday.com/news/nation/2005-07-18-cohabit-divorce_x.htm
[11] http://www.faithandvalues.com/tx/00/01/10/108/10844/
[12] http://www.kidsincommon.org/greenbookproject.php
[13] http://www.betterman.org/resourcelist5.htm

Child Abuse and Neglect

Each week, child protective services (CPS) agencies throughout the United States receive more than 50,000 reports of suspected child abuse or neglect. In 2002, 2.6 million reports concerning the welfare of approximately 4.5 million children were made.[14] Investigations into these claims revealed that approximately 896,000 children were found to have been victims of abuse or neglect - an average of more than 2,450 children per day. An average of nearly four children die every day as a result of child abuse or neglect (1,400 in 2002).[15]

Rape

According to the U.S. Department of Justice, somewhere in America, a woman is raped every 2 minutes. One of the most startling aspects of sex crimes is how many go unreported. The most common reasons given by women for not reporting these crimes are the belief that it is a private or personal matter, and the fear of reprisal from the assailant. Approximately 28% of victims are raped by husbands or boyfriends, 35% by acquaintances, and 5% by other relatives. (Violence against Women, Bureau of Justice Statistics, U. S. Dept. of Justice, 1994). The FBI estimates that only 37% of all rapes are reported to the police. U.S. Justice Department statistics are even lower, with only 26% of all rapes or attempted rapes being reported to law enforcement officials.[16]

The consequences of rape are not always physical though, and are not always immediate. 80% of rape victims will suffer from chronic physical or psychological conditions over time. (Strategies for the Treatment and Prevention of Sexual Assault.1995) Rape survivors are also 13 times more likely to attempt suicide than crime victims and 6 times more likely than victims of other crimes. (Rape in America: A Report to the Nation, 1992) 26% of women with bulimia nervosa were raped at some point in their lives. The mental health costs of sexual assault victims are very high; studies have shown that 25-50% of rape and child sexual abuse victims receive some sort of mental health treatment as a result of the victimization. (Miller, 1996) Overall, rape has the highest annual victim cost of any

[14] http://pediatrics.about.com/od/childabuse/a/05_abuse_stats.htm
[15] http://www.socialworkers.org/practice/children/0405snapshotb.asp
[16] http://www.paralumun.com/issuesrapestats.htm

crime. The annual victim costs are $127 billion (excluding child sex abuse cases). This is followed by assault at $93 billion per year, murder (excluding arson and drunk driving) at $61 billion and child abuse at $56 billion per year. (Miller)[17]

HIV/AIDS

There are more than 1.2 million people in the U.S. estimated to be living with HIV/AIDS and 25 percent of them are undiagnosed and unaware of their HIV infection. Women account for a growing share of estimated AIDS diagnoses in the U.S. In 1985, women represented eight percent of AIDS diagnoses; by 2005 they accounted for 27 percent. There are currently more than 300,000 women living with HIV/AIDS in the U.S. African-American and Hispanic women make up a combined 24 percent of the U.S. female population, yet their communities represented an estimated 79 percent of HIV/AIDS cases among women in 2005. In 2005, the estimated rate of HIV/AIDS cases among African-American women was nearly 23 times the rate for white women, and the rate of HIV/AIDS cases among Hispanic women was nearly six times the rate for white women. In 2004, HIV/AIDS was the leading cause of death among African-American women aged 25-34. The majority of women diagnosed with HIV in the U.S. are of childbearing age. Each year, more than 6,000 HIV-positive women in the U.S. give birth.[18]

Worldwide over 22 million people have died from AIDS. Over 42 million people are living with HIV/AIDS, and 74 percent of these infected people live in sub-Saharan Africa. Over 19 million women are living with HIV/AIDS. By the year 2010, five countries (Ethiopia, Nigeria, China, India, and Russia) with 40 percent of the world's population will add 50 to 75 million infected people to the worldwide pool of HIV disease. There are 14,000 new infections every day (95 percent in developing countries). HIV/AIDS is a "disease of young people" with half of the 5 million new infections each year occurring among people ages 15 to 24. The UN estimates that, currently, there are 14 million AIDS orphans and that by 2010 there will be 25 million.[19]

[17] http://sa.rochester.edu/masa/stats.php

[18].http://www.thewellproject.org/en_US/Tools/PressReleases/WS_Fact_Sheet_FINAL.pdf

These aforementioned statistics point to the dysfunctional behavior that is eating away and destroying the fabric of families like a menacing cancer. How do we, and in particular women cope with and defeat this dysfunctional behavior? Deuteronomy 28:1-14 says that if we want to have peace and not dysfunction in our families, than we should not follow other gods and serve them. Our husbands or any individual, including ministers, should not become gods in our life. Neither should the wife become a trophy god to her husband. God is a god of balance and fairness, and He is not a respecter of persons.

We must not forget that He instructed the husband to love his wife, as Jesus loved the church and gave his life for it (Ephesians 5:25). A careful reading of Ephesians 5, and not just a selective reading that endorses one's ego or need to be on top, would reveal that we are instructed to *submit ourselves to one another in the fear of God* (verse 21). As Christ loved the church and presented it without spot or blemish, men as the head of the household must love their wives and be a *reflection of Christ's love*. The husband's responsibility is to love and cherish his wife (verses 28-29).

How a man treats his wife is a reflection of how that man sees himself. If a man is abusive towards his wife physically, emotionally, verbally, or spiritually, he is demonstrating that inwardly, he feels a sense of self-hatred and unworthiness (verse 28). This man is not in alignment with God's Word or will for his life. If we follow the instructions of verse 21 and *submit ourselves one to another in the fear of God and not man*, we would have wholesome, loving, heterosexual relationships.

As men leave behind the ill advice that society and their parents have taught them and join their wives in *submission to God* (verse 31), then the two truly would become one flesh unto God. Matthew 18:19-20 NIV explains this concept as follows—"Again, I tell you that if two of you on earth agree about anything you ask for, it will be done for you by my Father in heaven. For where two or three come together in my name, there

[19] http://www.until.org/statistics.shtml

am I with them." This is true unity of the flesh [spiritual unity], obeying God's Word— not the actual exchange of marriage vows or the changing of one's surname.

The enemy's job is to prevent us from submitting to God as Lord over our lives and becoming one in the flesh. If he can divide the man and the woman, he can prevent them from being in unity with one another, and *stop the transmission of the Word of God from generation to generation.* It is when we come together as one flesh, [whether as husband and wife, or the church in general], that we are able to take back what was stolen from us in the Garden of Eden, and eat of the tree of life.

Unfortunately, many of the supporters of verses, I Cor 14:34-35 fail to acknowledge that Paul did not forbid women from ever teaching in the church. They fail to see that Paul was speaking to a Corinthian group of women *whose law* ("...They are not allowed to speak, but must be in submission, *as the Law says")* at that particular time forbade women from speaking in the church. Paul was intelligent, well-educated, and possessed wisdom. He had respect for the individual's culture and its laws and used that knowledge to his advantage. He in fact was able to escape death and spread the gospel in Rome because of his understanding and articulation of Roman law and his ability to speak Greek and Aramaic (Acts 22, 23).

Proof that Paul was not against women teaching the Word is clearly stated in Romans 16:3-5 wherein he expressed gratitude to his fellow worker, Priscilla *who taught Apollos*, the great preacher (Acts 18:24-28). She and her husband, Aquila, had a church in their house and taught many, according to Romans 16:3-5 and risked their lives. Paul also mentioned other women like Phoebe, who held positions of responsibility, worked in the church and was a great help to Paul (Romans 16:1-2 NIV). Mary, Tryphena, Tryphosa and Persis were the Lord's workers (Romans 16:6,12), as were Euodia and Syntyche (Philippians 4:2-3NIV).

Paul "commended" these women, which means according to Webster's dictionary that he represented them as worthy, qualified, and desirable. Another definition of the word commend according to Webster, is to commit to the care of others, to entrust.[20] In Romans 16:1-2 NIV, Paul asked that they receive Phoebe in the Lord in a way *worthy of the saints,* and to give her anything she may need, for she had been of great help to him and many other people. Paul greeted Junia as a fellow prisoner and referred to her as *of note among the apostles* (Romans 16:7).

Let us look closely now at how Jesus loved the church. Remember, Jesus came to fulfill the law. Jesus is part of the Trinity and there is no higher criterion than what Jesus established while he was here on Earth. How did Jesus, how did God see women and their role in society? How were they used by God, what roles were they anointed to fill according to the Bible? The following are some of the many roles assigned to women:

- First mentioned in the Bible *as a reflection of God*, to be fruitful, multiply, replenish *and take dominion of the earth* (Genesis 1:27-28)
- As a "help meet" in the form of a wife (Genesis 2:18)
- Mothers, homemakers, and entrepreneurs (Genesis 4:1, I Samuel 1:21-28, 2:20-21, Proverbs 31:10-31, Matthew 1:18)
- A woman used by God to bring a word of correction to her husband (Genesis 21:8-13)
- An abused Egyptian woman who God promised to make her seed into a great nation (Genesis 21:9-18)
- Prophetess (Exodus 15:20, Judges 4:4, II Kings 22:14, Joel 2:28-29, Acts 2:17-18)
- Dancers, song writers (Exodus 15:20, Judges 5:1,12, 11:34, 21:21, Jeremiah 31:13, Matthew 14:6)
- An Ethiopian [Cushite] woman who God protected and caused her enemy to be plagued with leprosy (Numbers 12:1-12)
- A former Canaanite prostitute who made it in the Hall of Fame and became an ancestor of Jesus (Joshua 6:22-25, Matthew 1:5, Hebrews 11:31)

[20] http://dictionary.reference.com/browse/commended

- Messengers, students and teachers (Judges 4:4-5, Ruth 3, Matthew 28:7-10, Luke 10:38-42, John 20:16-18, Romans 16:3-5)
- Judges, leaders, mediators, counselors, advisers, planners, peacemakers, financial supporters of the church, beautiful women, persuasive speakers, counselors, negotiators, intellectuals, intercessors, queens, planners, courageous risk takers, discerners of spiritual truth, meek and teachable individuals, (Judges 4:4-5, Esther 2:15-18, 4:12-17, I Samuel 25:25-42, I Kings 10:1-10, I Kings 17:7-24, Acts 16:14-15, 16:40)
- A Moab woman and an Israelite woman who were faithful followers of God's Word, hard workers, strategists, God chasers, truth seekers, covenant keepers, lovers of God and not man, risk takers (Ruth 1-4)
- A woman used by God to save the life of a king (I Samuel 19:11-17)
- A woman used by God to avert a war preempted by her foolish husband (I Samuel 25:25-38)
- An obedient and faithful widow that God provided a way for her to be self-sufficient, and enabled her to leave a business and inheritance to her two sons (II Kings 4:1-7)
- A great woman of tenacious faith and discernment that made room in her life for God, and believed that God was able to bring dead things to life. A mother who demonstrated her faith by not giving up on her dead son until God breathed life back into him. (II Kings 4:8-37)
- Builders, construction workers (Nehemiah 3:12 NIV)
- Mourning and cunning women used by God to redeem the body of Christ (Jeremiah 9:17-25)
- A Canaanite woman of great faith that would not be denied because of her nationality, who received a healing from Jesus for her daughter (Matthew 15:22-28)
- Witnesses, persecuted followers, and prisoners (Matthew 28:8-10, Acts 8:3)
- A watchman (Luke 2:37-38 NIV)
- A Jewish woman important enough for Jesus to interrupt his teachings with the disciples, and worthy enough to be

loosed not only on the Sabbath, but the remaining six days of the week from all manner of bondage and oppression (Luke 13:10-17)

- A poor widow who gave more financially than all the wealthy aristocrats (Luke 21:1-4)
- A sinful Samaritan woman at the well that Jesus offered everlasting life, who became a conduit for other Samaritans to accept Christ (John 4:4-30, 4: 39-41)
- A forgiven, adulterous, Gentile woman freed from the bondage of sin (John 8:2-11)
- Recipients of the Holy Ghost on the day of Pentecost (Acts 1:8, 1:13-15, 2:1-18)
- A husband and wife ministry team (Acts 18:2,18:18, 18:24-28, Romans 16:3-5)

In Luke 10:38-42, Jesus embraced Martha's hospitality as a homemaker, but he told Martha that *only one thing was needed* and Mary, who sat at Jesus' feet as a student, had made the better choice. The virtuous woman in Proverbs 31:10-31 is given praise not because she is a passive, simple, naive woman that stays at home, obeys her husband and is uninformed when it comes to world events. Instead, she is given praise because she is a hard worker.

Not only is she is a homemaker, but she is also a professional woman who is a real estate investor, manufacturer, seamstress, and a philanthropist. She has beauty on the outside and is well clothed, attractive, but more importantly she has an internal robe of righteousness. She has clothed [robed] herself with beauty on the inside that touches the lives of others. She has left a legacy of righteousness and accomplishments through Christ for others to emulate.

These are the types of women Jesus was attracted to. Jesus saw and treated women as equals, much to the dismay of the Sanhedrin, Sadducees, Pharisees, and the disciples. These were not silent woman sitting in the church or hidden by a veil at home waiting for a commandment from their husbands, or some man in authority.

Jesus saw women as being multifaceted, able to multitask,

and he anointed them to do virtually every role a man could do. He made room for them in his life. People who are great make room in their lives for that which is important. When the woman with the issue of blood touched him, he stopped his meeting with the boys to heal her. Although there were throngs of people touching him, Jesus was able to tune into her immediately because she made a *faith connection.* Jesus perceived that virtue had gone out of him. She pulled it out of him by making a faith connection, and she *pleased God.*

Hebrews 11:6 says that "without faith it is impossible to please God." It is not about our outward appearance, the robes we wear, our gender, how many Bible verses we know, or favor with man. It is about faith in God and obeying his "proceeding Word" (Matthew 4:4). When we do this and follow the two great commandments (Matthew 22:36-40), God cannot help but make room for us, regardless of who we are. We are supposed to be followers of Christ first, and obedient to God's order above man's social order.

In Romans 3:3 the question was asked, "…Shall their unbelief make the faith of God without effect? Continuing with verse 4, the question is answered as follows, "God forbid: yea, let God be true, but every man a liar, as it is written, that thou mightest be justified in thy sayings, and mightest overcome when thou art judged."

What is it in the human spirit that causes us to always question- who will sit on the right or left of Jesus? I question as well the incessant concern about who will be the head, who will be on top. What is in our makeup that causes us to hunger for control and power? Why do we constantly judge and look for who is right or wrong? I wonder why there is not a line for those who want to be first to submit, to be the servant as Jesus commanded us to be. Instinctively, as Christians, we must know that if we make a faith connection, God will be with us and that greater is He that is within us, than he that is in the world.

There are player-haters in the world that don't want you to sit at Jesus' feet, or touch him for yourself and make a faith connection. These player-haters inwardly really don't want you to search for that Lost Coin, the Kingdom of God, within you.

They want you to bow down to them, and they want to keep you in submission to them. Unfortunately, sometimes these teachers may clothe themselves as do-gooders, family members, friends, or even ministers of the gospel. They may feel threatened, like David's wife (II Samuel 6:16-23) when they see your overwhelming attraction to God and not them.

Unfortunately, in many parts of the world including the United States, women are seen often as metaphorically unclean. They are seen as second-class citizens, to be seen and not heard. Sadly, even today in some parts of the world, women must clothe themselves in black, and are imprisoned behind a veiled burqa, which is an Afghan garment that covers a woman's body from head to toe with only a grille or netting, which allows the wearer to see out. I don't know whether men can fully grasp what it feels like to go through your entire life veiled and imprisoned behind a real or imaginary robe, and to have your thoughts and ideas discounted, or worse, not even considered, because they come from the mouth of a female.

Remember, Peter was admonished to call no one "unclean" (Acts10: 11-35). God is not a respecter of person." Surely, if God will speak through a donkey to bring about correction and the sparing of a misguided life (Numbers 22:21-36), he will speak through a woman to proclaim his Word to all nations. The gains of Pentecost are being lost. Jesus said, "It is finished!" and the veil was torn to signify that we could individually come before Christ and ask for redemption and salvation. Both men and women were in the Upper Room and received the baptismal of the Holy Spirit and were given the injunction to be witnesses and to feed Jesus' sheep (Acts 1:8, 1:13-15, 2:1-18).

It is time for the body of Christ to usher in Jesus' return by getting our hearts, minds and lives right so that Jesus can return. We can't usher in Christ until we accept his Word, believe it and make room in our hearts, our minds, our churches, and our institutions for women and the socially "unclean." God is Spirit, and they that worship him must worship him in spirit and in truth.

If we truly want to be fruitful and multiply, then we must operate in the spirit realm and wait for God's instructions. Our partnerships, networking, assignments of officers, church officials, etc. must be spiritually deliberated and not based on what we see with our eyes, or what has been done traditionally. We must ask the question, "What would Jesus do?" and follow the counsel of God after much prayer and spiritual discernment.

Remember too, it was *to women that Jesus appeared to first* after his resurrection, and appointed them to go to the disciples and *tell them* that Christ is risen. He appeared first to the unclean according to society, to Mary Magdalene, whom he had cast seven devils out of, and the other Mary (Matthew 28:1-7, Mark 16:9). When Jesus later appeared to the disciples, he rebuked them for their *lack of faith*, their stubborn refusal to believe the eyewitness accounts of the women, and for their *insistence that the women's account were full of nonsense* (Mark 16:14, Luke 24:11 NIV).

Let me reiterate, Christ deemed women important enough to appear to them *first*. In Matthew 9:12 NIV Jesus said, "It is not the healthy who need a doctor, but the sick." I believe that Jesus recognized that women were special and needed in the body of Christ. I believe Christ knew that they are faith seed carriers, capable of carrying truth within their bellies when no one around them knows that they are pregnant, but willing to endure criticism until the baby, the harvest, the gestation period is complete. These women didn't have to put their hand into Jesus' nail holes to know that He was the risen Christ.

Isn't it amazing that the disciples who walked and talked with Jesus, saw countless miracles performed and were constantly with Him, did not recognize Jesus after the resurrection (Luke 24:13-29 NIV)? Even though Jesus expounded on the scriptures from Moses to the prophets during their *7-mile walk* to Emmaus, the two disciples were still unable to recognize the Savior. Even John, the one that Jesus loved and we see pictures of him laying on Jesus' breast, didn't recognize Him. In contrast, when the angels told the women that Jesus had risen, they believed it instantly without questioning or seeing him (Matthew 28:5-8).

I believe Jesus appeared to women first because he knew they would believe the angel's report before they saw Christ, unlike the disciples who had to see him with their own eyes. I believe women are very much needed in the body of Christ, not just as a help meet to their husbands, but also to the church and society at large.

Even science tells us that men and women are distinctly different. Women are more right brain thinkers and men, of course, use their left brain more. Men are created to be more rational, if they don't see it, feel it, manipulate it; it's not real to them. It wasn't until Jesus manipulated [broke] the bread, that the disciples recognized him (Luke 24:30-31). Whereas women are more intuitive, able to believe that something is true even though all the dots don't connect. Women in general have been given a special ability to believe that though something appears dead; it can come back to life again.

Do you remember what Jesus told the disciples after they had fished all night and encountered a situation of barrenness? Jesus told them to cast their nets on the "right side." Perhaps Jesus was telling them that after they had done all they could do from a human point of view, [analytical left brain thinking] they needed to embrace the intuitive, right side of their brain. That is, they had to seek a higher source, that higher intelligence, that all-seeing, all-knowing force that I call God, Jehovah Jireh that *knows where all the fish in the world are*. I think Jesus was also telling them that they needed to become one with their "help meet," which the female, the intuitive part of the marital relationship personifies.

Perhaps this is why men don't like to ask for directions. Perhaps they can't help it. It may be programmed in their brains that they can do it themselves. What may have been designed as a survival instinct may also serve as a detriment to men, and cause them to come up barren after many years of fishing, of working on a dream, a project, if they are unable to ask for intuitive help.

If God has designed and programmed males and females to conceive and bring forth fruit in the natural and the spiritual when we come together as one, wouldn't it be foolish to not ask for directions or to leave women and God out of major decisions? I question how many more wars could have been averted if women were involved in major political decisions (I Samuel 25:25-38).

Accordingly, our churches and political and social institutions should reflect women in all levels of authority and positions of power. If our premise holds true that males and females are made in the image and likeness of God, (Genesis 1:27-28) even though both have unique characteristics, the commandment to be fruitful and multiply cannot be fulfilled until there is a marriage in the spiritual realm. When we become the bride of Christ, whether male or female, Jew or Gentile, then we have fulfilled the commandment to be fruitful and multiply, and both men and women will be reflected at all levels of authority and positions of power in the church and social institutions. It is then that we become one and can experience true Pentecost (Acts 2:1-11, 2:17-18, 10:34-35).

Unfortunately, the church has been slow to embrace and accept God's Word and the role of women in the church. Luke 16:8 says that, "…the children of this world are in their generation wiser than the children of light." In the secular world, we see evidence of change as we witness emerging female powerhouses like Secretary of State Dr. Condoleezza Rice, Speaker of the United States House of Representatives Nancy Pelosi, and United States Presidential Candidate Hillary Rhodam Clinton. Incidentally, Dr. Rice speaks fluent Russian and, with varying degrees of fluency, German, French and Spanish.

But the church is still reluctant to understand and respond to God's Word. The church seems at times more concerned with having church, than being the light of the world, as Jesus commanded us to be. Instead of the government being upon our shoulders, and the church being the lender, we are grappling for faith-based grants to pay our church bills.

Instead of governmental leaders seeking out Christians who have a plan like Joseph to end famine, poverty, discrimination, HIV/AIDS, and any other social ills that might surface, some pastors become puppets of the government and not true followers of Christ. We, as Christian leaders, are commissioned by God to be peacemakers. The government is supposed to be upon our shoulders. We are supposed to be the *head* and not the *tail*!

Ultimately, we are responsible for our own salvation. We must guard our hearts, (Proverbs 4:23 NIV); ask God for wisdom and discernment as we study and read the Word, and make sure our teachers' instructions line up with the Word of God. Even Jesus when he was called "Good Master" deferred to God and would not take credit or glory from the Father. God is a jealous God. He wants us to have no other gods before him. And yes, this does include our husbands. God should be the head of our house, our consciousness, and our churches. All that we do should be in accordance with God's Word. In the family, the husband is the head in the natural realm, but God is the head in the spirit realm, and every knee, every social order must bow to him.

How this translates is that we as married women must be in subjection to our husbands, only if our husband's will lines up with the will of God. Your husband has no heaven or hell to put you in. Don't fear man, but fear God, who is able through his Word to divide asunder soul and spirit, and is a discerner of the thoughts and intents of the heart (Hebrews 4:12). Only God has the power and the authority to put you in heaven or snatch you from hell.

When Jesus told the woman with an infirmity, "thou art loosed," he meant just that. There is no affliction that God cannot heal! God admonishes women in Isaiah 32:9-20 to rise up and usher in righteousness if we want to have peace in our homes and cities. To understand this passage, we must listen with a *spiritual ear* to what God is saying to women, *but also to the nurturing, loving, and giving side within men*. It reads as follows:

> Rise up, ye women that are at ease; hear my voice, ye careless daughters; give ear unto my speech.
> Many days and years shall ye be troubled, ye careless women: for the vintage shall fail, the gathering shall not come.
> Tremble ye women that are at ease; strip you, and make you bare, and gird sackcloth upon your loins.
> They shall lament for the teats, for the pleasant fields, for the fruitful vine…

> Until the spirit be poured upon us from on high, and the wilderness be a fruitful field...
> And my people shall dwell in a peaceable habitation, and in sure dwellings, and in quiet resting places... And the work of righteousness shall be peace... *Blessed are ye that sow beside all waters...*

God is telling us to make ourselves uncomfortable, and to forsake the pleasures of this world, to sacrifice our fleshly desires so that we can bring about a greater good for all of mankind. God wants us to sow beside all waters [all nations and types] to bring forth peace and righteousness (v.20). When we submit ourselves to God, his spirit will be poured upon us, and we are then empowered to make the wilderness a fruitful field (v.15).

When women, as caretakers, gird sackcloth upon their loins and take up Jesus' cross (v.11), there will be lamenting "for the teats, for the pleasant fields, for the fruitful vine" that we represent to society (v.12). Sackcloth is rough and uncomfortable material. Be prepared for resistance and opposition when women rise up and say to men, "I am more than a sexual object, a caretaker of children and a bed partner to my husband." When women rise up and set their affections on Christ, there will be great lamenting and opposition.

This act will place women in a wilderness type of experience (vs.12-13), but the Word says that this discomfort is necessary to bring forth a peaceable habitation (vs.15-18) so that we can be healed. In Revelation 12:14 God's promises to give the woman, who represents metaphorically the church, two wings to fly into the wilderness *where she is nourished.* When we have endured the chastisement of God and have endured our wilderness experiences, then we enable the lame to be healed. Hebrews 12:12-13 NIV puts it this way, "Therefore, strengthen your feeble arms and weak knees. Make level paths for your feet, so that the lame may not be disabled, but rather healed."

God is admonishing us to rise up and usher in righteousness if we want to have peace in our homes and cities. He is telling us to make ourselves uncomfortable, and to forsake the pleasures of this world, to sacrifice our fleshly desires so that we can bring about a greater good for all of mankind. God wants us to sow beside all waters, that is, all nations and types, to bring forth peace and righteousness. When we submit ourselves to God, his spirit will be poured upon us, and we are then *empowered to make the wilderness a fruitful field.*

Men and women are three-fold beings. We are mind, body and spirit. God has placed us on this Earth to do more than live in palaces, populate the world with children and be a trophy to our spouse. God's will is that men and women would *become one with Him,* and that we would bring forth *spiritual fruit and multiply* the Earth for the kingdom of God (Genesis 1:27-28). God wants us to take back what was stolen from Adam in the Garden of Eden.

It is incumbent upon us as believers to usher in the new kingdom, the spiritual kingdom where there will be no Jew or Gentile, male or female, black or white. The battle is not between the sexes or the races, but between the seed of the enemy and the seed of Abraham. The enemy wants to put division between men, women and nations so that we lose our focus and allow the enemy to come in and steal our vineyard, our seed, which Christ redeemed for us on the cross.

Why are we so concerned about being politically or socially correct? Where are the intrepid individuals, men and women alike, that will listen to the inner voice of God and not man? Where are the modern day Josephs? The Harriet Tubmans, the Abraham Lincolns, the Mahatma Gandhis, the Rosa Parks, the Dr. and Mrs. Kings, the Mother Teresas, the Nelson Mandelas, who are willing to make themselves uncomfortable so that they can bring forth a more peaceable habitation for the world? Are you listening to that still small voice within you like Samuel, so that you can respond to God and say, "Here I am, I'll go and do your will? I'll gird myself with sackcloth and make myself uncomfortable so that I can bring forth peace in my home and in this world."

I challenge you to think about what you are doing with the god and goddess in you! Are you willing to rise and be healed, and heal others in the name of Jesus? The Bible, God's Word is sackcloth for both men and women, but it is also healing to our mind, body and soul. We must taste and see that the Lord is good!

God is our Jehovah Jireh, he is our husbandman. If we live in fear that our husbands will leave us because we don't maintain a certain weight, or have dinner on time, or be totally in agreement with him, then we must use discernment and question first - does his request line up with God's Word? Is it fair, are we being taken advantage of?

If it is not fair, and we are not being abused, our role according to scripture is to submit, but we must cast our cares upon the Christ. As we go to God with our concerns in prayer, he will cause our husbands to change their minds and their hearts towards us. God will give us the wisdom, like he did with Abigail, to deal with a foolish husband. If our husband's request does not line up with the will of God, then we must speak out with diplomacy, like Sarah with a word of correction, knowing that God will intervene and make the crooked places straight (Genesis 21:8-13).

Please note what I mean by "with diplomacy." This does not mean that if you are married to an ill-tempered man that is in a rage that you speak what you feel is right. Timing is everything and you must be wise and discerning and know when you should speak a word of correction. There are times, however, when your mate may be in a rage and you feel you must run for your life. I recommend during these times that you speak to that enemy by pleading the blood of Jesus out loud, and take off running like David ran from Saul. Please note, I am not being humorous, but I am speaking what I know has saved me from dangerous situations with men.

I want to underscore that submission to one's husband does not mean staying in a situation where the wife or children are being physically or emotionally abused, and/or prevented from serving God. For the sake of your soul, your life (and your children's if there are any), you must seek a divorce from a husband of this type.

God is ultimately our husbandman, whether we are male or female, Jew or Gentile, black or white, and we should have no other gods before him. He is our Jehovah Jireh, our rock and our shield. He will take us through the valley of the shadow of death. His rod and staff will comfort us, and He will take us to the place where goodness and mercy shall follow us. He will take us to the house [consciousness] of the Lord, the house of shalom forever.

In a nutshell, if we want to be the *head* and get to the palace, whether male or female, we must learn this one of many lessons that Joseph mastered and practiced - obedience to God's Word, his will, regardless of whether we are abased or esteemed, single or married. God is not a man that He should lie. Since He said that we are the *head*, then we must fulfill our part of the covenant by obeying all of his Word in order to bring it into manifestation.

To the reader, learn to treasure your wilderness experiences. It is in those barren places that you can find God, and He can cause you and your seed to become a great nation as He promised to Hagar during her wilderness experience. Like Joseph, what looks like evil on the surface, ironically serves to strengthen, reward and empower you as well as others.

We must follow the advice found in Isaiah 54:1-3 and begin to sing in our barren places. It reads as follows:

> Sing, O barren, thou that didst not bear, break forth into singing, and cry aloud, thou that didst not travail with child: for *more are the children of the desolate than the children of the married wife*, saith the LORD. Enlarge the place of thy tent, and let them stretch forth the curtains of thine habitations: spare not, lengthen thy cords, and strengthen thy stakes; For thou shalt break forth on the right hand and on the left; and *thy seed shall inherit the Gentiles, and make the desolate cities to be inhabited.*

The reason we sing is because we have already won the battle, and our reward is greater than those who appear to be fulfilled in their lives, their marriages, workplaces, etc. These verses are particularly encouraging to those who feel forsaken and forgotten. At the cross, Jesus said, "It is finished!" Our role is to believe God, do his will and follow the Word.

When we obey his Word, He will cause our barren places to

spring forth with everlasting waters. Out of our bellies will flow rivers of living water that will impact generations to come (John 7:38). We will then leave a legacy that enables the lame to be healed as we make ourselves uncomfortable and gird our loins [our spiritual reproductive capacity] with sackcloth [the Word of God]. When we die to self, and express the Christ within us, then God will bring forth a peaceable habitation in our homes, and in this world. When we do this, then the following verse from Revelation 7:17 will manifest in our lives, "For the Lamb which is in the midst of the throne shall feed them, and shall lead them unto living fountains of waters: and God shall wipe away all tears from their eyes."

Step 4
Forgiving Your Abusers

So when Joseph came to his brothers, they stripped him of his robe- the richly ornamented robe he was wearing-and they took him and threw him into the cistern. Now the cistern was empty; there was no water in it…

And he [Joseph] kissed all his brothers and wept over them.

Genesis 37:23, 45:15 NIV

What do you do when your cistern is empty and you are stripped of your clothes? If you keep living, sooner or later you will go through some experience that will strip you of your dignity, your sense of who you are. It may happen to you as a child in the form of incest, abuse, discrimination, or maltreatment or it may occur in your teens, or during your adult years. Sooner or later, something will happen that unnerves you and threatens or takes away your strength and/or resources. It can be a health challenge, job loss, death, difficult marriage, or divorce. There is a myriad of events that can happen that make you question your relationship with God, or question whether God has forgotten you. You may even get to the point where you question whether there is a God at all.

In one form or another, and often from the church pulpit, we hear that we are the *head* and not the *tail*, but our circumstances belie this truth. It seems illogical to say that we are the *head*, when everything that we see and experience says just the opposite. Joseph had a dream that he would be the *head*, yet he was hated by his brothers and thrown into an empty place where there was no water, no resources for him to draw from. Joseph pleaded for his life, but his brothers turned a deaf ear, and calmly sat down and ate their meal. Joseph, who was sent to inquire about his brothers' welfare, was now in jeopardy of losing his own life.

Similarly, Jesus was later sent to inquire about his brothers - the bruised, the broken-hearted, the Mary Magdelenes of the world. He suffered an ill fate in the flesh at the hands of his brothers, but rose from the dead in three days so that we might have a right to the tree of life. Like Joseph, what the enemy meant for evil, God turned it around for the good of all mankind.

It seems so cruel that one's own flesh and blood would want to see you dead. Although we judge and question the humanity of Joseph's brothers, how different are they from you and me? How many times have we let jealousy, bitterness, and hatred get the best of us even after we were "saved?" How can a spouse that took a covenant to love "to death do we part," tell you that they no longer love you; they want to trade you in for a younger, thinner, or richer model? How can a child that you nursed at your breast tell you that they don't need you, you are no longer relevant, or they hate you? How can an employer tell you weeks before retirement that you are being let go and you will lose your pension as well? These are the cisterns, the dry places devoid of resources that we are sometimes placed in.

Although they stripped Joseph of his clothes, like Jesus had been stripped of his, they could not strip Joseph of his anointing. They said to one another, "We'll see what comes of his dreams." No one can strip you of your anointing. You are sealed until the day of redemption according to Ephesians 4:30. Remember, the enemy is after the spiritual seed within you as it is passed from generation to generation.

Two questions were asked in Rev.7: 13, concerning the great multitude of believers that no one could number from all nations in Rev.7: 9 as follows: "What are these which are arrayed in white robes? And whence came they?" The answer, found in Rev.7: 14, was that these are God's servants, "These are they which came out of great tribulation, and have washed *their robes*, and made them white in the blood of the Lamb."

Unfortunately, as you go through life, there are people who will try to strip you of your robe, your anointing, your gift, your joy, your enthusiasm, and the Holy Spirit that is within you. They want to uncover you and remove the seal [your robe] that God has placed on those that belong to him. They want to prevent you from washing your robe and becoming that new creature that has closed the door to defeat, and has become the *head* of their emotions, relationships, finances, health, and their spirit man.

These naysayers have given up on life or their dreams, and

sometimes will do everything in their power to ensure that your dreams don't manifest. Sometimes, they may appear well intentioned and say remarks like, "I'd like to give you a little advice." At other times, they can be downright vindictive and evil like Joseph's brothers were. Remember to guard your heart, for out of it flows the issues of life.

Parenthetically, let me say that they stripped Jesus of everything except the loincloth that covered his reproductive organs. It in interesting that as barbaric as they were, they did not touch his loincloth. You see, they could not touch or strip it because it stood for us, his seed that would come forth out of his belly, "the living water," (John 7:38, Rev.7:17). The blood of Jesus that flowed down from his body covered us, the living water, and no devil could interfere with the plans that God has for his seed.

When the destroyer saw the blood that covered Jesus' loins [his spiritual reproductive capacity], it had to pass over and preserve us, his seed. We are the living water that Christ died for, the redeemed. We are the ones who have been fed by and washed in the blood of the Lamb as we submit and follow God's will (Revelation 7:17).

My struggle from Boston's inner city housing projects to where I am now was not without intense opposition. At times, I encountered resistance from family members and friends who were not supportive. I had to endure cruel, hurtful remarks intent on keeping me in a position of poverty, self-doubt, and negativity. I was told that black people shouldn't strive for the higher things in life. I was warned as well that if I did finish college, no one would give me a job.

Oftentimes, those who are in the pit don't want to see you leave because it is a reflection on them. They may attempt to make you feel guilty for wanting to excel, for wanting to use the gifts that God has given you. As long as your peers, relatives, and associates are in the same pot of inadequacy, self-doubt and destructive thinking and behavior, your taunters feel *they* must be okay. The adage, misery loves [miserable] company is definitely applicable here.

The other lie that is told to women is that the more you

become educated; you lessen the number of suitable marriage partners. As I excelled and matriculated through a private high school, private college and graduate school, I had to endure stares and taunting remarks from the "haves" who wondered what a "have not" was doing in the best schools in America. And yes, even some of my good Christian brothers and sisters told me that instead of pursuing college and a lucrative job, I should desire a mediocre job and just serve God in the local church as a Sunday School teacher.

I too, at times have found myself in an empty, lonely pit like Joseph, with no water, no subsistence, no options, *no one to turn to but God.* All Joseph could do in the pit was to look up. Although his brothers had abandoned him for dead, they could not take Joseph's anointing from him. Like Dorothy in the Wizard of Oz, the witch couldn't take Dorothy's shoes, - Dorothy's anointing, from her. Although they stripped Joseph outwardly, they could not touch his ability to look up and draw from the everlasting water within him of the Holy Spirit.

This dry, barren, empty place was a critical turning point that launched Joseph towards his destiny of being the *head.* If he had not endured the pit, he would have never become the *head.* It is ironic that at Joseph's lowest point, God is the closest to him, turning what the enemy meant for evil into good. God used a group of heathen Ishmaelites to launch Joseph into his destiny of being the head of the Egyptian nation.

The Bible says not to despise small beginnings. God is everywhere, evenly present. His will is that we have life and it more abundantly. But we must do our part like Joseph, and taste and see that the Lord is good. Like Joseph, we must endure hardship, the dry empty places in our life like a good soldier, knowing that if we faint not, we shall overcome and be the *head* as God has preordained for every believer since the beginning of time. Like Joseph, God will make our enemies and our "inner me's" [enemies inside of us], our footstool. We, too, will gain the victory over those cistern experiences that we thought would overwhelm or destroy us.

Like a disciplined soldier, Joseph learned to obey God's Word, and practiced love and forgiveness. The Word says that by this will all men know that you are my disciples, *when you love one another.* As Joseph fulfilled the covenant to forgive and love one's enemies, God fulfilled His contractual side of the covenant to protect, bless, prosper, and consequently made Joseph the *head.*

We too, as believers, must follow Joseph's example if we want to escape the cistern places where we are presumably left for dead, in order to become the head of our emotions, thoughts, relationships, finances, health, the spirit man, etc. When we are stripped and abandoned, it is then that we must look up to Jesus and affirm that by *his stripes we are already healed and declare that no weapon formed against us shall prosper.*

We must live out the words found in Matthew 6:33, which says, "But seek ye first the kingdom of God, [the will of God] and his righteousness [right living]; and all these things shall be added unto you." When we put God first in our lives, then the "things"- the houses, spouses, children, health, wealth, and most important, the shalom of God are added.

Jesus was a master psychologist that understood the importance of forgiveness. He told the woman at the well that he would give her living water so that she would never thirst again, but he took her *through a process of cleansing* her past first so that she might be whole. To the woman caught in adultery, he likewise told her *she was forgiven,* and not to sin anymore. To the man that was sick with palsy, he healed him, told him to pick up his bed and walk and that *his sins were forgiven.* Jesus was more concerned about cleansing the heart, the inner garment rather than the outer robe.

As a therapist, I have spent considerable time with individuals, groups, and families in counseling sessions dealing with issues of addiction, alcoholism, poverty, teen pregnancy, abortion, death, marital discord, etc. Overwhelmingly in these meetings, the emotions of guilt, anger, loneliness, hatred, pain, and unforgiveness were present and had to be confronted in order for healing to take place. The problem with secular counseling is that therapists are traditionally trained to leave out the God factor.

Ironically, this is the very factor that contains the healing balm. For example, you can teach someone in a counseling session how to deal with past incidents of rape or incest, but this is cleansing the outer robe, the outer man. Until you get to the inner man and show that individual how to release their hurt and anger and *forgive and pray for their predator*, that individual will always remain a victim. They become tied to their predator and *they can't pick up their bed of affliction* and be healed, they can't *go and sin no more*, and they can't let go of their addictions.

That's why the woman at the well had five husbands, one affair, and if it hadn't been for her encounter with Jesus, she would have been working on her seventh relationship. Metaphysically, the number 7 is completion. This woman would have spent her entire life going from man to man, because she never had a real encounter with Christ, the Living Water, and she never forgave herself of her past destructive behavior and belief systems.

I wonder if this woman at the well had been abused or raped as a child or young woman, disrobed by someone that held a position of trust in her life. I wonder what caused her to feel that she was entitled only to leftovers, a belief system that told her she could not have a husband of her own who would love, cherish, and be faithful to her alone. Whatever the reason, it did not matter to Jesus, he told her to go and sin no more. As a spiritually mature Christian, we must go and sin no more. Even if we are placed in unjust situations, retaliation is not the solution. Sin only begets more sin.

We have a part to play in our healing, our recovery from sin, pathological behavior and generational curses. Erroneously, some churches teach that sin must be removed by casting it out. This is only a half-truth. Our recovery involves more than simply getting a demon cast out of us. A belief system like this frees the individual from personal responsibility to pick up their bed of affliction and walk. Casting out devils is simply casting out a belief system that says you were not made in the image and likeness of God. It is an erroneous thought system that says God has not given you a special robe with gifts and talents that are unique to you, and that you are entitled to the blessings of

Abraham.

Once you hear The Word and accept the new birth that Jesus gives, you must then walk these truths out in your life. Yes, you must cast out the negative belief systems, but you also must renew your mind and thoughts daily by studying and applying God's Word to your life. When you do this and become a follower of Christ, then you can go and sin no more. You are then empowered through Christ to put that liquor bottle down, put those unhealthy foods down, refuse the needle in your arm, and stop any type of negative, pathological, destructive behavior that takes away the peace from your mind, body and soul.

We have matured when we can take the next step, like Joseph, and forgive and kiss all of our brothers [our enemies and inner me's] and weep and pray over them. Joseph demonstrated true love at its finest. Remember also that Jesus *wept not over himself, but Jerusalem* before he executed the greatest blessing to mankind, the shedding of his blood so that we would have the right to inherit eternal life.

This weeping may appear on the surface to be non-masculine, childish, a sign of weakness, and serve no purpose other than to release emotions or pain. Remember, too, that God's promise in his Word is that weeping may endure for a night, but joy would come in the morning. God also promises in Rev. 21:4 the following:

> And God shall wipe away all tears from their eyes; and there shall be no more death, neither sorrow, nor crying, neither shall there be any more pain: for the former things are passed away.

If we want to be the *head*, then we must obey God's Word like Joseph, and release to God our tears, our hurt, our pain, so that He can supernaturally move on our behalf and remove us from the pits in life that attempt to ensnare us. You can vent in a therapy session until you are blue in the face, but only God can give us a supernatural catharsis that cleanses the mind, body and soul. Remember, He alone is able to divide the soul and spirit.

Even if we only have a mustard seed of faith remaining, we must use that and trust that God's Word is true. We must declare like Jesus, Joseph, and Job that "though He slay me, yet shall I serve Him." We must learn to take personal responsibility for our actions, [pick up our bed of affliction] - forgive, pray for, love, and kiss our enemies. When we do this and give God the praise in spite of our circumstances, it is then that God will show up in our cisterns, give us the *living water* we so desperately need, and make us the head over all of our enemies and inner me's!

Step 5
Staying the Course

> The Lord was with Joseph, and he was a prosperous man; and he was in the house of his master the Egyptian… The lord blessed the Egyptian's house for Joseph's sake; and the blessing of the Lord was upon all that he [Potiphar] had in the house, and in the field. And he left all that he had in Joseph's hand…
>
> Genesis 39:2, 5-6

Notice the order of the scripture, and how the blessing came upon the Egyptian master's house. First, the Lord was with Joseph, meaning Joseph did not forsake the teachings of his youth or his Abrahamic covenant with God. He obeyed his parents and those in authority over him. Secondly, because Joseph walked with God, Joseph was a prosperous man. Everything Joseph touched prospered. And lastly, Joseph affected those around him so much that even his heathen master's house was blessed. His master was blessed in the house and in the field because of Joseph.

When you walk with God, you are a prosperous person, it doesn't matter whose house or pit or city they put you in - you prosper where others fail, because God is with you and you have his spiritual DNA in you, so you must prosper! If the Lord is with us, He will make our way safe, successful, and prosperous, regardless of where we are - in a back alley, prison, the Twin Towers, or on Wall Street. The Word says in Psalm 91:7, "A thousand shall fall at thy side, and ten thousand at thy right hand; but it shall not come nigh thee."

You know that you have spiritually matured like Joseph when your supervisor can place total responsibility of the firm, office, or business in your hands. When you operate in a spirit of excellence, inadvertently you end up doing a better job than the owner of the company could do himself. Your supervisor [oppressor] becomes hard pressed not to leave you in total control of his estate, because to do otherwise would mean a tremendous loss of revenue and profit.

Historically, I am convinced that one of the reasons that

African Americans better survived the horrors of slavery and its after-effects in comparison to how Native Americans survived the Great Migration had to do with the slaves' ability to adopt what is disdainfully called an "Uncle Tom" mentality. The dictionary defines an Uncle Tom as "A Black person who is regarded as being humiliatingly subservient or deferential to white people". [21]

I believe that many of these Uncle Toms had Joseph-like spirits and should be regarded as heroes and martyrs who sacrificed their self-dignity and their lives at times so that their families and the black race could survive until the institution of slavery and its remnant Jim Crow laws were abolished. I see these Uncle Toms as modern day Josephs that believed that if they faithfully served their white masters and brought them gain, their master would not kill them or their progeny. I believe that somewhere in the Uncle Toms' minds, there was a belief that they could touch the humanity of their masters or mistresses and receive some small compensation.

Lydia Parrish, in her book, *Slave Songs Of The Georgia Sea Islands* recounts the many slave songs that helped African Americans to psychologically endure the brutality and inhumanity of slavery. Spirituals, like "Steal Away to Jesus" and "Swing Low Sweet Chariot" not only brought comfort to the slaves, but also contained hidden messages letting them know that emancipation would come soon. This emancipation was not just upon their transition to heaven, but also to let the slaves know clandestinely when a slave revolt would take place, or when passage had been cleared for them to escape through the Underground Railroad.

This ability to defer one's own needs, desires, and in the case of slaves and oppressed African Americans, to risk their lives and seemingly give up their self respect by acting in such a debasing and deferential role comes from a maturity deep within. Out of the brutality, inhumanity, and ashes of slavery, there arose a belief in a monotheistic God and an adoption into the family of Abraham by faith. Christianity served as an anchor that

---

[21] http://dictionary.reference.com/browse/Uncle tom

later transformed the hearts and minds of the oppressors, and African Americans were eventually emancipated. Out of the ashes we now see those who were considered the *tail*, now becoming the *head* as we witness and marvel at the accomplishments of Oprah Winfrey, Tiger Woods, President Nelson Mandela, President Barack Obama and many others of African descent.

I want to digress and illustrate the metamorphosis of the caterpillar into a butterfly to explain spiritual maturation using biological concepts. In the larval stage, you see caterpillars everywhere if you are out walking on a warm spring day. They are right under your feet, and many succumb to death easily by being stepped on by humans, or eaten by other creatures. A butterfly in its pupal stage is barely noticed and it looks like it is dead, but it is in its *protective cocoon*.

Once it emerges as a butterfly, however, it is apparent to everyone how this despicable worm-like creature has become a beautiful, winged masterpiece that can fly above its enemies of the past and easily elude them. Even though you are already a butterfly in truth, you must go through this pupal, seemingly dead stage. It is this threshing floor experience that transforms one into the mature adult God has preordained since the beginning of time.

This is how it is for the seed of Abraham in the spirit realm. We may start life in a lowly manger, a ghetto, a dysfunctional household, or experience some things in life that bring us to a worm-like condition, but if we die to our old self and endure the cocoon process, we will emerge victoriously over our enemies, like Joseph did. The key is to go through this metamorphosis when no one notices you, and continue to do what is right, even when you have been wronged. Eventually, you will be noticed and your gift will bring you before great men (Proverbs 18:16).

The metamorphosis takes place on the threshing floor of our bitter life experiences. It is where the wheat is separated from the chaff. It is where we learn to die to the old self, so that the new self can emerge. This processing, this threshing floor experience is where most people jump ship. Like the Hebrews, they wish for the good old days back in Egypt, even if they were enslaved there.

Why do we, like Esau, sell ourselves short or give up our birthright for a piece of meat, a one night stand, a hit, or one more drink? I wonder why we so easily walk away from our Abrahamic birthright for some perceived immediate need that can't be delayed for a later time. Is it because we love the creation more than the Creator? What causes us to keep going around the same mountain?

Paul, with great consternation, summed up this dilemma as follows: "For the good that I would, I do not: but the evil which I would not, that I do" (Romans 7:19-25). Flesh and blood can only do so much and we should strive with every ounce of our being to solve our own problems. That's why God gave us a brain and a heart of compassion. But there are some battles that are spiritual, and we must engage in these battles with spiritual weapons.

Paul (and Joseph) resolved that these were spiritual battles, and Paul gave the following counsel on how to resolve them in II Cor 10:4-5.

> For the weapons of our warfare are not carnal, but mighty through God to the pulling down of strong holds; Casting down imaginations, and every high thing that exalteth itself against the knowledge of God, and bringing into captivity every thought to the obedience of Christ.

They solved these problems by choosing to become yoked with the spirit of Christ. When you become yoked with Christ, you can then become transformed into that new creature like the butterfly, and emerge victoriously over your enemies of the past. Your enemies of the past are looking for you in the pit, your little cocoon, but you are now flying high, mastering earthly and celestial places with Jesus on your side.

It is interesting to note how the butterfly gets out of its cocoon. I want to share how this process happens in the natural; because there are some amazing parallels to human spiritual and emotional maturation that I feel God has hidden in the metamorphis of the caterpillar.

In this side-by-side interpretation of this transformation, I will explain how the yoking together with Christ brings about the metamorphis in our Christian lives. In the book, "Butterfly and Moth," by Paul Whalley, he describes this process in the natural in detail. After the caterpillar becomes yoked with its chrysalis (cocoon), it breaks free from it as follows:

> **FIRST STAGE**
> Once the insect has completed its metamorphis and is ready to emerge, [from its cocoon] it begins to pump body fluids into its head and thorax. This helps to split the chrysalis [cocoon] along certain weak points, so that the adult insect can begin to force its way out with its legs.

Likewise in the spirit realm, before we can emerge from our physical, emotional, financial or mental pit, we must pump the Word of God - i.e., *wisdom,* into our mind, our heart and our mouth. The Word of God must first of all be heard and discerned spiritually. As we acknowledge our shortcomings, the Word enables us to confront our weaknesses. We must next use our mouth and the breath within our chest to speak into our life, and strengthen our legs so that we can run with our newfound vision as a son or daughter of Abraham (Habakkuk 2:2-3).

Jesus himself submitted himself to his parents and to the Word of God. Not only did he increase in wisdom and stature, but he also grew in favor with God and man. Jesus was about his Father's business of teaching and spreading the Gospel (Luke 2:48-52).

Sometimes, we wonder why we must go through certain pit-like experiences. We question whether we have done something to deserve it, but the Word tells us that this bruising of the flesh is necessary "so that the lame may not be disabled, but rather healed." It is through our suffering that our misery becomes a ministry and we can then empower those who are lame to be healed.

> **HEAD AND THORAX EMERGE**
> Once the skin of the chrysalis is broken, expansion can proceed more rapidly. Inflation is due not only to the body fluids in the head and thorax, but also to the air the insect takes in. Although

by now the antennae, head and palps [sensory organs for tasting food] are visible; the wings are still too soft and crumpled for proper identification.

As we enlarge our vision and inflate our knowledge, that is to say spiritual air or wisdom and discernment of the Word of God into our heads, - i.e., our spiritual minds or our hearts, we are still not ready to take flight. It is important to note that people still identify us in our pit-like condition. At this juncture, we must continue to grow in our secret place and guard our hearts. We are not fully mature at this point. This is not the time to announce to the world our vision, our destiny, and the prophecy over our life, or to start a worldwide ministry. We are still in a vulnerable stage of growth, and people still identify and see us as a worm-like creature. Even Jesus was not recognized in his hometown of Nazareth. They said of him, "can any good thing come out of Nazareth?"

We must study the Word like Joseph did, and submit ourselves to a God-ordained mentor and become a true disciple of Christ. II Timothy 2:15 reads as follows:

> Study to show thyself approved unto God, a workman that needeth not to be ashamed rightly dividing the word of truth.

COMPLETELY FREE

Having pushed its way out of the chrysalis, the butterfly's body now hangs free. At this stage, the butterfly's exoskeleton [the outside skeleton of all insects] is soft and still capable of more expansion. If, for any reason, the butterfly is damaged at this stage, or confined (perhaps by a thoughtless collector), complete expansion is not possible: all the parts harden and a crippled butterfly results.

In Matthew 12:43-45, Jesus warned listeners to be careful of possible fallout that may happen when you leave your prison, and your house [consciousness] is cleaned out. Jesus explained that it is easy to become complacent and lose sight of the fact that we may have left the door open for seven more devils to enter in.

Even though we are free and out of our pit, we must be careful whom we associate with and whose advice or counsel we lend our ear to. We must leave our prison buddies, our codependent friends with their addictive behaviors behind us, *less we become hardened and go back to our old ways* or worse yet, fall more deeply into sin. It is important as well to beware of thoughtless collectors who want to market or manage your gift for profit or gain. We must remain in prayer like Jesus, and seek his counsel and spiritual discernment and let him order our steps.

STEADILY GROWING WINGS

With the butterfly now out of its pupal skin, the most important actions are the ejection of stored wastes from the abdomen and the expansion of the wings. As it forces blood from its body into its wings, a butterfly or moth will usually hang head-up so that the pull of gravity helps to stretch crumpled wings.

In order for our wings to expand and prepare us for flight, we must consciously rid ourselves of negative thoughts, belief systems and relationships that we have accumulated over the years in our abdomen, our gut. As we shed our old skin, [our old robe, our old sense of who we are] we rid our abdomen, our belly, our gut, of stored wastes by daily asking God for forgiveness and strength to die to our negative, self-defeating behavior.

And most importantly, we must forgive our enemies, real or perceived. We must be willing to endure the process of cleansing. We must stay the course. Enduring is more than just speaking it; *we must go through the dying process of releasing negative habits, thoughts, relationships, and false belief systems.*

We as believers grow our new wings by consciously yielding to the pull of the Holy Spirit. When we do this, out of our bellies will flow rivers of living water, according to John 7:38-39. This cleansing and yielding to the mind of Christ allows us to produce the fruits of the spirit, which then allows us to stretch and mature so that we can develop spiritual wings to rise above our enemies.

Revelation 12:14 explains this concept as follows:

And to the woman [the church] were given two wings of a great

> eagle, that she might fly into the wilderness, into her place, where she is nourished for a time... from the face of the serpent.

In our wilderness experiences, we must allow God to anoint our head with oil [redeem our minds] so that our cup [our lives] will run over with goodness and mercy (Psalms 23:5-6). As we hold our head up towards Christ, let his mind richly dwell in us, and let the blood of Jesus cover us, we will receive spiritual nourishment. Our wings will then expand and we will gain the victory over our enemies.

An interesting parallel, and a sobering one, is that when Jesus hung on the cross, *his blood was forced from his body* by the pull of gravity, and as he grew his spiritual wings, he became a conduit for us to grow ours. A Middle English interpretation of the word, "conduit," is "a fountain."[22] Jesus, by taking our sins on Him and expelling them, became a living fountain for us and paved the way for living water to flow from our bellies.

> **BECOMING ITS FULL SIZE**
> By now, the veins in the wings have almost filled with blood, and it is possible to see the wings visibly expanding. The expansion must take place fairly rapidly, or the wings will dry before they have reached their full size. If this happens, the butterfly may be too crippled to fly.

As the new you becomes apparent to those around you, be careful that you don't let others pull on your new found wings, [your influence and expansion] and attempt to cripple you. It will be apparent to those around you that you are about to launch into a new career, relationship, or non-addictive behavior. There will be many that want to pull on you and get on board your ship for a free ride.

Of note, after Jesus' resurrection when he appeared first to Mary Magdalene (John 20:14-17), she attempted to touch him, but Jesus told her not to do so. Mary wanted to keep him on Earth, close to her, but Jesus had not yet ascended into heaven.

---

[22] http://dictionary.reference.com/browse/conduit

He was under command to fulfill the scriptures, undergo his full transformation [become hardened] so that the entire world could touch Him through our receipt of the Comforter, the promised Holy Spirit.

Continue to study the Word and use discernment as to who you let lay their chest on yours. And, of course, you must continue to fast and pray, less you become tempted. You must follow the instructions that Jesus gave the disciples, that is, to be continually in the temple [in a state of praise] praising God (Acts 1:4-8, 1:12-14; 2:1-18). Remember, Jesus said that "your body" is the temple of the Holy Spirit, (I Cor 6:19) not a building per se. God wants us to praise Him in *our temple at all times*, not one day a week in a building on Sunday.

WAITING TO FLY

After a period of about ten to twenty minutes, the wings reach their full size. The butterfly now waits for its wings to harden properly before it attempts to fly. Then, after an hour or so, and some preliminary opening and closing of its wings, the butterfly takes to the air. It usually flies straight to a plant or other food source for its first meal.

They say the darkest hour is just before dawn. As you wait for the fulfillment of this final stage of development, know that weeping may endure for a night, but joy cometh in the morning. By now, you have had many test runs, you have been practicing your gift, you have received some small rewards, but the big one, payday, is right around the corner. Prepare yourself to sit at the banquet table, you have earned it - you have kept the faith, you have stayed the course!

As the butterfly eats its first meal and prepares to continue the cycle of life, you too must continue to eat from the tree of life and prepare yourself to mate and develop spiritual seed so that others may be set free and come into God's kingdom. By staying the course and mentoring others, you are ensuring that out of your belly, living water will flow for generations yet unborn.

After Jesus' resurrection he ate his first meal with the disciples and demonstrated through the breaking of bread that he wanted them to stay the course and break the bread of life, that is, the Word of God with all mankind so that the bruised and broken hearted would be set at liberty (Luke 24:30-53, Mark 16:14-18).

Step 6
Overcoming Sexual Temptation

...Now Joseph was well-built and handsome and after a while his master's wife took notice of Joseph and said, 'Come to bed with me!' ... And though she [Potiphar's wife] spoke to Joseph day after day, he refused to go to bed with her or even be with her.

Genesis 39:6-10 NIV

"If you got it, flaunt it!" is a popular expression in Western culture. The presumption is that your looks must be used to your advantage to get what you want. After all, the advertisers tell us that sex sells, so the logic follows that we must follow suit and use what we have to get what we want. We are inundated daily with messages that say, "Forget about your morals, who's looking, it's a dog eat dog world, your looks don't last forever, so use what you have to get what you want."

It is very tempting to use what is beautiful about you - your gifts, your talents, your intelligence, or the robe of your physical covering to get the supposed upper hand in a relationship. This is particularly so when the gift is of a physical nature and you are the underdog in the relationship. Joseph, however, did not yield to the temptation of Pharoah's wife. Even though Joseph's brother, Judah, freely married a heathen woman and used his daughter-in-law as a prostitute, Joseph's *spiritual DNA* would not let him sin. Joseph responded with the words, "...because thou art his wife: how then can I do this great wickedness, and *sin against God*?" (Genesis 39:9)

Joseph's primary concern was in pleasing God. Joseph's response exemplified a deep conviction, a belief that there is a God who is in charge of the universe, and that He is just and will vindicate the oppressed in due season. I believe that Joseph had learned through his cistern and near death experiences to deeply depend on God. Out of these tribulations had come a deep abiding faith in God, an intimate relationship that could not be shaken for a few minutes of fleshly pleasure.

Joseph also denied himself of favors; pleasures and promotions that I'm sure would have gone along with being the male concubine of Potiphar's wife. Joseph probably would have received the best food, clothing, trips, and relief from the baser and harsh duties associated with being a slave and running the captain of the guard's house. Joseph was not willing to give up his Abrahamic birthright. Although he had been stripped of his robe outwardly, he would not let go of his internal robe of oneness with God. The Bible says that:

> The fear, [i.e., the awe, reverence, love, respect, and the wonder] of the Lord is the beginning of wisdom: a good understanding have all they that *do his commandments…*
> (Psalm 111:10)

There is a special message in Proverbs 31:3 that is directed explicitly to men as follows: "Give not thy strength unto women, nor thy ways to that which destroyeth kings." In modern day vernacular, this message might be better understood if I said it this way, "Don't give your jewels to women." Simply put in the natural, if both males and females were chaste, there would be no occurrences of out of wedlock pregnancy, rape, or sexual molestation.

Cases of HIV, AIDS, and other sexually transmitted diseases would drastically be reduced and minimized from their present epidemic state. This advice, if properly understood and applied, would not only prolong a man or woman's life, but would cause one to become prosperous and leave an inheritance to their children's children.

The Bible cites numerous examples that exemplify this advice and show the folly of giving your jewels to undeserving women. Samson, a judge born to do a special work for God, let sensuality control his life and was almost ruined by Delilah. Lot battled carnality, but was saved because he mustered enough strength not to look back and did not become a pillar of salt like his wife. Job was also saved and received double for his trouble by ignoring his wife's denial of sexual favors and the tauntings from her to curse God and die.

Ironically, Solomon, the wisest man who ever lived, and

David, his father, who is known as the greatest king of Israel, both succumbed to the lust of the flesh. Solomon is said to have written most of the book of Proverbs, from which we get this warning above about giving one's strength to women. Centuries later, this warning still falls on deaf ears. The headlines are still full of presidents, ministers, those in high authority, as well as lay people who have fallen from positions of power, affluence and influence with family, society and friends because of their inability to harness and control their lusts and sexual organs.

This prophetic warning, however, does not let women off the hook. Remember, it takes two to tango. In the case of Joseph, it was Potiphar's wife who was in a position of power and influence. Unfortunately today, there are some women in positions of power that are dominating headlines as being the sexual aggressor and, yes, sometimes the predators of not only men, but also women and children.

If we want to be the *head* like Joseph, and get to our palace, [our place of shalom] then we must follow in Joseph's footsteps and learn from his experiences. Joseph's reaction to Potiphar's wife's advances was to flee the scene. Habakkuk 2:2-3, reads:

> ...Write the vision and make it plain upon tables, that *he may run* that readeth it. For the vision is yet for an *appointed time*, but at the end it shall speak, and not lie: though it tarry, wait for it, because it will surely come, it will not tarry.

Joseph had his vision, his dream, that he would be the *head, but he had to literally run with it*, endure hardship and wait for its *appointed time* to manifest in his life. It takes strength, wisdom, courage and God's grace to deny the flesh and run with the vision that God has given you. The Bible tells us to endure hardness as a good soldier (II Timothy 2:3). You must know that you are in a spiritual battle, regardless of how the enemy is disguised or robed in the natural.

Unfortunately, Joseph left his cloak, [his robe] behind. Although his cloak was used against him as evidence, Potiphar's wife, however, could not take his internal cloak of integrity, his vision from him. Joseph's strength remained intact, because he guarded his heart and refused to give his strength to her. His vision remained intact as well; sitting unperturbed like a mother hen sits on her nest waiting for the appointed time of birth. Like Joseph, we must guard our hearts, our visions until the appointed time.

This battle is more than about a few romps in the hay; this is a spiritual battle over the seed of Abraham. We, as survivors of the African Diaspora, the Jewish holocaust, and Christian battles, must realize that the fight is not about us, but about the seed that is within us. We must guard our hearts, and know that we are carrying precious seed, "God's vision," and his plan for the redemption of mankind that must be passed from generation to generation. We must fulfill our purpose while we are here on Earth, and leave our imprint for all eternity.

Sex is a strong, natural drive, ordained by God to perpetuate the human race. The Word says that it is meant for the use of heterosexual married couples for mutual enjoyment, pleasure, and procreation. Proverbs 31 goes on to describe the other benefits of marriage, and why a man should seek to find a good wife. First of all, it explains that a husband will have no need for spoil. The word spoil is defined as "plunder." To plunder something is to take goods by force or wrongfully. Because this good wife is a wise woman, she knows how to satisfy her man so that he has no desire to look outside the marriage and take something that is not his.

Proverbs 31 details how a woman can affect and bring a positive change to her husband, children and neighborhood. Not only does she help the poor, but she buys land, is a manufacturer, importer, manager, farmer, seamstress, upholsterer, merchant and has a business that she can pass on to her children. This woman is known around town and is admired by all. A woman of this caliber would not have any difficulty finding another man if her husband was foolish enough to leave her for someone else. Although she is away from home at times, the heart of her husband does safely trust in her, and he expectantly waits for her return.

Like Joseph, she is God fearing, has a prosperous attitude, and whatever she does and touches, can't help but to excel and prosper. By putting God first, she, like Joseph, is able to possess the land. *This is how we too can inherit the land. This is how we can take back what the enemy attempts to steal from us*. Like Joseph, and Proverbs' virtuous woman, we must obey God and his Word. We must know within our inner core of being that God is our husbandman, and that He is a jealous God.

Joseph had a strong abiding love for God that enabled him to look past the lust and pleasures of the flesh, and say and understand that *the greater sin is against God.* Even though he was held in an unjust situation against his will, Joseph's integrity, character, and love were such that he would not deny God. This, to me, is a true demonstration of Joseph's love for God, not by vain words, or praises, but by his actions under pressure.

Under pressure in desolate and barren places, what is in us is expressed. As a sign of our spiritual maturity, if the fruit of our experience is "living water" like Joseph's was, then we are most assuredly on our way to the Promised Land. If we can endure hardness, temptation and criticism like Joseph did, then we are leaving a legacy by which all men will know that the Father is in us. Like the woman at the well, when they see the Christ within us, they will want to taste of the Living Water. They will know that we are a son or daughter of God when they see the shalom of God in our hearts and our lives.

The writer of Proverbs 31 ends by saying that favor is deceitful, and beauty is vain: but a woman that feareth the Lord, she shall be praised. If we want the praise of God, then we must follow the examples of these two mentors that held God in awe, and obeyed His commandments to love God first, and our neighbors as ourselves. Joseph was later rewarded for his obedience and sexual abstinence and was promoted as the head of Egypt. He was given a wife as well and eventually had two sons.

Step 7
Keeping Your Sanity

And Joseph came in unto them in the morning, and looked upon them, and, behold, they were sad. And he asked Pharaoh's officers that were with him in the ward of his lord's house, saying, "Wherefore look ye so sadly to day?"

Genesis 40:6-7

Joseph amazes me. He is definitely a unique, esoteric, Pollyanna character. Why would Joseph ask prisoners early in the morning why they looked sad? What did he expect their emotional demeanor to be - jubilant, ecstatic? After all, they were *in prison.* Most people in prison look and act sad, depressed, lonely, and feel forsaken. It is definitely not the penthouse suite at the Waldorf-Astoria.

Joseph was probably the first recorded *love child or moony* in the Bible. The unique quality about Joseph is that he let the child in him shine and have permanent residence within his heart, wherever he was. Whether abased or elevated, sunny day or dreary day, nothing disturbed Joseph's inner peace and joyful spirit. I marvel at Joseph's ability to take a "lickin' and keep on tickin." I also admire his ability to look beyond himself and have empathy and compassion for others while he himself was in prison.

Joseph had a choice; he could have become angry, bitter, resentful and selfish. He could have turned his back on God and said, "I won't let my light, my gift shine in this prison unless I'm on stage in front of all the lights and cameras." After receiving the divine interpretation of the chief butler's upcoming release and restoration to his position as the Pharaoh's butler, Joseph could have struck a deal and perverted his gift. He could have bartered an exchange of this information for a favorable release for himself.

Instead, Joseph said, by the way when you are restored, "… think on me when it shall be well with thee, and shew kindness, I pray thee, unto me, and make mention of me unto Pharaoh, and bring me out of this house" (Genesis 40:14). Joseph demonstrated humility and a knowingness that sooner or later, his time would come for release. I have to believe that Joseph had an inherent, unshakable, prophetic belief that God would eventually vindicate him and bring him to greatness. Joseph did not let anything disturb the calm of his soul, or his resolve to serve God with a joyful attitude wherever he was planted, whether justly or unjustly.

At the risk of being hurt, ostracized, or criticized, Joseph gave a straightforward and unfavorable interpretation of the chief baker's dream. Joseph did not hold back or whitewash it because it was not politically correct to predict the baker's death. Joseph was instead obedient to God and was not governed by the approval of men. Joseph could have also struck a deal with the chief baker as well. Joseph could have attempted to play God and ask for some concession from the chief baker to ward off his imminent destruction. But instead, Joseph was a straight shooter and was more concerned with gaining the sanction of God than man.

Another option Joseph could have taken was to squelch his gift. Joseph could have made the decision to not help anyone, because his gift was not setting him free. Sometimes, it is very tempting to hold back, become dismayed, and refuse to help others when we are in the pit ourselves. He also could have become envious, angry and depressed because others were getting blessed through his efforts, and he was not getting the credit for their success.

When we are in the pit, we must use our gifts like Joseph to emancipate others. It is important that we realize that it is not about us, but about God's precious seed that He is seeking and trying to reclaim. It is the "Prodigal Son," the "Lost Coin" that God is looking for, and using believers as conduits to save these lost souls. As Jesus went to the cross and hell to save us, we must be willing to suffer offenses like Joseph and Jesus to bring others to Christ.

Joseph was too busy helping others while he was in prison to feel sorry for himself and let a spirit of depression or loneliness overtake him. He held the key in his hands for his redemption, for his emancipation from his depressed circumstances. *The key was to use what was in his hands, his gifts,* to set at liberty those that were bruised and broken hearted around him. As Joseph, like Jesus, used his gifts, including the gift of spiritual discernment to set fellow prisoners free, his gifts made room for him and brought him before great people. Joseph eventually reaped what he had sown: he was set free, and made ruler over Egypt.

Joseph was not only gifted as a dreamer and interpreter of dreams, but he also was an embodiment of the fruits of the Spirit (Galatians 5:22-23). Wherever Joseph was planted, whether in the pit or the palace, he demonstrated love, joy, peace, long-suffering, gentleness, goodness, faith, meekness, and temperance. It was Joseph's obedience and his crucifixion of the flesh that caused God to be well pleased with him. Because Joseph had forsaken the lusts of the flesh and was a living testimony of God's goodness, Joseph was rewarded accordingly.

God promises to reward us greatly for our efforts. He tells us over and over that He is a good God and that He loves us with an everlasting love. Luke 12: 27-32 puts it this way:

> Consider the lilies how they grow: they toil not, they spin not; and yet I say unto you, that Solomon in all his glory was not arrayed like one of these.
> If then God so clothe the grass, which is to day in the field, and to morrow is cast into the oven; how much more will he clothe you, O ye of little faith?
> And seek not ye what ye shall eat, or what ye shall drink, neither be ye of doubtful mind.
> For all these things do the nations of the world seek after: and your Father knoweth that ye have need of these things.
> But rather seek ye the kingdom of God; and all these things shall be added unto you. Fear not, little flock; for it is your Father's good pleasure to give you the kingdom.

In Luke 11:13, God compares the love of an earthly father who is inherently evil, to his love for us to prove that He does love us and will not forsake us. I Cor. 2:9, tells us, "…Eye hath not seen, nor ear heard, neither have *entered into the heart of man* the things which God hath prepared for them that love Him." It is unthinkable, imperceptible to man what God has prepared for us. No matter how hard we try to think of or perceive what it is, it is beyond human comprehension.

In Mark 10:29-30 God again attempts to tell us the reward is great for those willing to follow Him. It reads as follows:

> ...There is no man that hath left house, or brethen, or sisters, or father, or mother, or wife, or children, or lands, for my sake, and the gospel's, But he shall receive an hundred-fold now in this time, houses and brethen, and sisters, and mothers, and children, and lands, with persecutions; and in the world to come eternal life.

In John 14:2-3, Jesus gives us this promise, "In my Father's house there are many mansions: if it were not so, I would have told you. I go to prepare a place for you... that where I am, there ye may be also." The exact meaning of this scripture is unknown. This is one of the many mysteries of the Bible. Where is this place that He is preparing for us? Does it mean we shall literally be with him in heaven? Where is heaven? Jesus did say that we would do greater things than He did, because he was going away. Does this mean while we are here on Earth, our minds will start to use that 90% of the brain that we don't use to do greater things, or will it be done by faith? Are the mansions symbolic of higher states of consciousness?

Is the Earth considered one of the mansions of God in the universe? If so, what other mansions are out in space? These are questions that make you say, "Hmmm" as man still discovers other planets in this galaxy. I marvel that in 2006, man has launched a spaceship to Pluto and it will take *nine years* to get there. What is incredulous to me is not that man has done it, but that it will take nine years to get there.

I've digressed not to showcase the awesomeness of the Earth and the universe, but the awesomeness of God, the creator of the universe. James 4:14 says that our life is "... a vapor, that appeareth for a little time and then vanisheth away." Somehow, for a brief moment in eternity, we spend our life on Earth and then we leave. Out of Job's pit-like experience, God questioned

Job in chapters 38 as follows:

> Then the Lord answered Job out of the whirlwind, and said, Who is this that darkeneth counsel by words without knowledge? Gird up now thy loins like a man; for I will demand of thee, and answer thou me. Were wast thou when I laid the foundations of the earth? declare, if thou hast understanding. Who laid the measures thereof, if thou knowest? Or who stretched the line upon it? Whereupon are the foundations thereof fastened? Or who laid the corner stone thereof...Or who shut up the sea with doors, when it brake forth, as if it had issued out of the womb... Who provideth for the raven his food? When his young ones cry unto God, they wander for lack of meat.

God is not trying to get answers from Job, but to demonstrate the limitations of man's knowledge of the universe's creation, the Earth's natural order, and the animal kingdom. We are finite beings in an infinite world. God used Job's ignorance of the universe's natural order to reveal his ignorance of God's moral order. If Job did not understand how God's physical creation was formed and operated, how could he possibly understand God's mind and character? There is no standard or criterion higher than God himself by which to judge. God Himself is the standard. He is the Alpha and the Omega. Our only option is to submit to His authority and rest in His care.

One thing, however, I can say that what is clear to me about the above passage from John 14:2-3, is that where Jesus is, there we shall be. I don't know how the Earth was formed, but I do know that you can't have order, design, beauty, and an intelligent creation without an intelligent, loving, wise Creator. I accept by faith and revelation in my spirit that Jesus is the Son of God and that he came to Earth suffered and died, and left his Holy Spirit as a comforter. I believe that Jesus abides with us whenever we acknowledge God as the great "I AM," which is interpreted as the great creator of the universe, the Alpha and the Omega.

We, as believers, may not have the answers to existential questions, but by faith, we must follow in Job's and Joseph's footsteps when we are being held hostage in negative, depressing situations, if we want to get to the palace. As Joseph used his gifts to deliver a word to the prisoners, we must use whatever is in our hands, continue to hone and master our skills and talents, seek God's Word and stand on it until our redemption manifests in the natural and/or spiritual realm.

We must be willing to obey God's Word and learn to endure hardship until we are able to emerge from our prison. The choice is ours to make, we can buckle down, trust and obey God and continue to bless others through the use of our gifts while we are in the pit. Or alternatively, we can keep going around the same mountain wasting many years that could have been productive and fruitful during our internship here on Earth. It is only after we go through this threshing process that we can get to the palace, that place of shalom.

Getting to this place of shalom is by no means easy in today's society. Statistics point to the fact that Major Depressive Disorder is the leading cause of disability in the U.S. for ages 15-44. It affects approximately 14.8 million American adults, or about 6.7 percent of the U.S. population, age 18 and older in a given year. While Major Depressive Disorder can develop at any age, the median age at onset is 32. It is more prevalent in women than in men.[23]

Suicide statistics are just as staggering. In 2004, 32,439 (approximately 11 per 100,000) people died by suicide in the U.S. More than 90 percent of the people who kill themselves have a diagnosable mental disorder, most commonly a depressive disorder, or a substance abuse disorder. Four times as many men as women die by suicide; however, women attempt suicide two to three times as often as men do.[24]

Statistics concerning substance abuse and other causes of death are alarming as well. The leading causes of death in 2000 were tobacco (435,000 deaths; 18.1% of total US deaths), poor diet and physical inactivity (400,000 deaths; 16.6%), and alcohol consumption (85,000 deaths; 3.5%).[25] Illicit drug use is

---

[23] http://www.nimh.nih.gov/publicat/numbers.cfm#MajorDepressive
[24] http://www.nimh.nih.gov/publicat/numbers.cfm
[25] http://www.drugwarfacts.org/causes.htm

associated with suicide, homicide, motor-vehicle injury, HIV infection, pneumonia, violence, mental illness, and hepatitis. An estimated 3 million individuals in the United States have serious drug problems.[26]

Statistics concerning an aberrant growth in the U.S.' prison population are equally startling and distressing. "Marc Mauer, in his *Americans Behind Bars: A Comparison of International Rates of Incarceration* (1991), was among the first who called attention to the fact that the United States has higher per capita rates of incarceration than many countries in the world. Sample headlines regarding Mauer's observations were "*America, the Land of the Imprisoned*" (Santa Barbara News-Press, February 20, 1992), "*The World's Top Jailer*" (USA Today, February 12, 1992) and "*A Dangerous Place to Live*" (St. Louis Post-Dispatch, February 11, 1992). On February 22, 1992, Boston Globe reported that few statistics about the United States are more startling than the growth of the prison population during the quarter-century since Americans abandoned the war on poverty. The Houston Chronicle (February 17, 1992) concluded that a potential human resource is being wasted. That is the real crime."[27]

Public Safety, Public Spending: Forecasting America's Prison Population 2007-2011 projects that "state and federal prisons will swell by more than 192,000 inmates over the next five years. This 13-percent jump triples the projected growth of the general U.S. population, and will raise the prison census to a total of more than 1.7 million people. Imprisonment levels are expected to keep rising in all but four states, reaching a national rate of 550 per 100,000, or one of every 182 Americans... The number of women prisoners is projected to grow by 16 percent by 2011, while the male population will increase 12 percent."[28]

Statistics like these should make it abundantly clear that societal, familial, judicial, penal and moral reforms are desperately needed in the United States. The remedies involved

---

[26] http://www.drugwarfacts.org/causes.htm

[27] http://en.wikipedia.org/wiki/Incarceration

[28] http://www.pewpublicsafety.org/pdfs/PCT%20Public%20Safety%20Public %20Spending.pdf

in healing these individuals are extremely complicated, time consuming, and expensive. Simply thinking good thoughts, or substituting a good thought for a bad one, guarantee healing. Neither does substituting a positive behavior for a negative one, promise healing or a sense of shalom. The threshing process can involve an inward battle with self as well as an outward battle with our perceived enemies. The battle can be a physical one involving your physiology as you try to lose or gain weight, detox from alcohol, nicotine or an addictive prescription or non-prescription drug. It can be a mental, emotional or spiritual battle as you try to change the tapes that constantly play in your mind from childhood and throughout life that tell you that you are not good enough, you're dumb, stupid, the wrong color, shape, size, gender, etc.

The list of self-deprecating thoughts, feelings, and statements can seem endless at times, and may cause some to consider ending their life. But God promises to never leave us alone! In spite of how distraught we may feel, we must encourage ourselves like David and realize that greater is He that is within us, than he that is in the world. We must stand on the Word that knows that there is nothing too hard for God. (Genesis 18:14) As we draw nigh to Him, He will draw nigh to us and prove to us that *the battle is not ours, but the Lord's!* (II Chronicles 20:15).

It is this interplay of where we leave off and God takes over that we must master. This can be particularly difficult for Christians who think that Christianity means that they must be perfect. We must not in times of distress and depression take the course that Judas took. Suicide or the pursuit of perfection is not an option. The Bible says that there is no sin that God will not forgive us from, save that of blasphemy against the Holy Ghost (Matthew 12:31), which is basically ascribing to Satan the works of the Holy Spirit. We must cast our cares, our worries, our sins, upon the Christ, and go free as He commanded in I Peter 5:7. God wants to forgive us of all sins. Are we willing to let go of them so that He can cleanse us and set us free?

We must remember that Jesus said he would not leave us comfortless. He told us that the Holy Spirit would be our Comforter when we invite him into our life. Jesus also told us that by his stripes, by the shedding of his blood, *we are already healed.* Spiritual battles and strongholds must be fought with spiritual weaponry. In Ephesians 6:13-20 we are told to gird ourselves, *to robe* ourselves as follows:

> Wherefore take unto you the whole armor of God that ye may be able to withstand in the evil day, and having done all to stand. Stand therefore, having your loins girt about with truth, and having on the breastplate of righteousness; And your feet shod with the preparation of the gospel of peace; Above all, taking the shield of faith to quench all the fiery darts of the wicked. And take the helmet of salvation, and the sword of the Spirit, which is the word of God: Praying always with all prayer and supplication for all saints; And for me, that utterance may be given unto me, that I may open my mouth boldly, to make known the mystery of the gospel, For which I am an ambassador in bonds; that therein I may speak boldly, as I ought to speak.

During times of despair, depression, loneliness, and seemingly hopelessness, the following verses from Isaiah 49:15-16 NIV have gotten me through the midnights in my life to daybreak:

> Can a mother forget the baby at her breast and have no compassion on the child she has borne? Though she may forget, I will not forget you! See I have engraved you on the palms of my hands; your walls are ever before me.

May these verses give comfort to those who feel they have been forsaken, unwanted, forgotten, abandoned at birth, disrobed, or stripped and left for dead in a barren place. Know that God loves you, *He has engraved you on the palms of his hands, you are ever before Him* and He has already counted every hair on your head. You are not an accident to Him. He loves you with an everlasting love! Luke 12:6-7 reads:

> Are not five sparrows sold for two farthings, [pennies] and not one of them is forgotten of God? But even the very hairs of your head are all numbered. Fear not therefore: ye are of more

value than many sparrows.

Consequently, let us not forget to call forth, to invoke the blood of Jesus to cover us during times of distress, despair, loneliness, depression, and uncertainty. God promised us that when He saw the blood, that the destroyer would pass over us and would not harm us (Exodus 12:13). The redeeming blood of Jesus has cleansed us already. His rod [The Word] and his staff [the Holy Spirit] are there to comfort us.

He has already prepared a table of bounty before us in the presence of our enemies. He will anoint our heads with oil. He will give us understanding of his Word and a supernatural enablement to defeat the enemy even in the face of death. Our gift will make room for us in spite of our enemies. Our cup will run over with joy, and out of our bellies will flow living water for future generations. Surely, goodness and mercy will follow us; not pain, suffering, and depression as we dwell in the house of the Lord, that place of shalom wherever we find ourselves, abased or esteemed. The Word says that God is omnipresent - there is nowhere that we can go and not have His presence of peace, if we make room and invite Him into our lives.

To the reader, wherever you find yourself today - in prison, in a difficult business meeting, or in a cancer ward, it doesn't matter where you are, Jesus will also make room for you and stop what He is doing to heal you when you make a faith connection. When you make room for God in your life, He will step in and occupy your space.

In the physical realm, whenever a vacuum is created, something will automatically step in and fill the void. If you cut your finger, your blood will automatically rush to the area and fill the void. Your blood in the natural realm is constantly circulating throughout your body every 23 seconds, cleansing, healing, replenishing, renewing and strengthening your body. That's why in the wilderness, you see some plants growing and thriving. In ghettos as well, if the blood of Jesus, [the proper nourishment] is there and the Word tells us that God is an omnipresent God, you will also see individuals thriving and prospering despite the odds.

In the desert, there are underground water springs that nourish certain plants that are built to survive in the wilderness. In the book, *The Pursuit of Happyness*, by Chris Gardner, this principle of underground water springs was demonstrated when a single father was able to live in a subway underground public bathroom with his young son, and they were able *to thrive* despite the odds. God is omnipresent, everywhere evenly present, and when we tap into Him, He will make room for us and supply our needs.

Consequently, when you go through your valley of the shadow of death, there is no need to fear any evil. Use your gifts that God has given you. They are redemptive and have been placed in you so that you can be successful and thrive despite any obstacles you may face in life. God's promise is to be there with you and to provide you with goodness and mercy so that you can dwell in a state of shalom during your time of adversity.

In summary; in the midst of your storm, know that you are not alone. God will provide a Joseph for you as well that will come into your life in the morning with a prophetic or rhema word that will reveal to you a way of escape, and a plan for your life. God is not limited in the methods He will use to provide a way for our vindication. God may also provide an Ebedmelech, [someone who is a foreigner, or someone of a different race or social class] who will advocate a release for you, just as He did for Jeremiah in chapter 38:6-13. If you have been unjustly placed in a literal prison, your Joseph, your Ebedmelech, your exoneration, may show up in the form of a DNA test that proves that you were not at the crime scene.

As you continue to hone your skills, obey God's Word and receive wise counsel, it is only a matter of time before you get that call, the friend, the advocate, the test or report that beckons you to a higher level.

Step 8
Vindication

...But when all goes well with you, remember me and show me kindness; mention me to the Pharaoh and get me out of this prison. For I was forcibly carried off from the land of the Hebrews, and even here I have done nothing to deserve being put in a dungeon.

...The chief cupbearer, however, did not remember Joseph; he forgot him.

Genesis 40:14-23 NIV

Prisons are not necessarily a physical building that confines an individual. A prison can be a mental or emotional state of being that confines you within your mind. You can live in a mansion in Beverly Hills and be in prison. You can be married to someone who is rich and famous, or poor and lowly, and still be in a prison. A physical condition, a difficult marriage, a drug addiction or an illness can keep you in bondage. The death of loved ones, divorce, loneliness, or lack of friends or only opportunistic friends who associate with you for what they can get, can be a source of anguish and pain. Old age and a decaying body can be an imprisonment to you as well.

Regardless of what type of prison you may find yourself in, know that according to God's Word, weeping may endure for a night, but joy cometh in the morning. Joseph's success in overcoming his imprisonment lay in his ability to adopt an Esther attitude that enabled him to survive and thrive, and help others while in prison. It was Queen Esther that during a time of persecution of her fellow Jews declared a fast and encouraged her countrymen to pray and give God the glory before the victory was won.

Joseph realized too that this was an attack of the enemy and that he was facing spiritual warfare. Like Job, he had done nothing to deserve his imprisonment. Like Esther, Joseph's attitude was, "If I perish, I perish, but I will not deny God and will serve Him whether abased or esteemed." The question inevitably arises as to how long one must stay in their prison, and what purpose it serves.

The timing of our release is two-fold in nature. As faith believers, there are some things that we have control over, and others that are totally up to God. We do have control, however, over how we react to our imprisonment. We can choose to take another drink or a hit, engage in an argument, victimize a child, pick up a prostitute or lie down as one, and prolong our imprisonment, or we can seek treatment and ask God for His strength and anointing to resist the challenge. The processing, the threshing floor experience is necessary. This is the refinement stage. It is important not to fight it, or ask God to remove the bitter cup (Matthew 26:39), but for *grace* to go through it.

When you adopt an, "if I perish, I perish" attitude like Esther and Jesus and go through your imprisonment, you have just *taken possession of the land, you have reclaimed the title to the land* according to the Abrahamic covenant. You have concurred with the Word that says that the Earth is the Lord's and the *fullness* thereof. You have taken back what the enemy has stolen not only from you and your ancestors, but your natural and spiritual descendants, yet unborn. To take this step, you must have a keen awareness and the spiritual acuity to realize that the battle is not about you, but it is about your seed as a manifestation of the seed of Abraham.

When you praise God anyway, just as Job, Joseph and Jesus did, you have defeated the enemy. You acknowledge that yes, this is a miserable place, but you make the best of it and give God the glory. You have defeated the acronym of *FEAR*— "false evidence appearing as real." Remember that faith is the substance of things hoped for, the *evidence of things not seen.* What you have done is substituted false, vain imaginations with positive, life affirming imaginations. You have taken the invisible things and called them forth to confirm with God's will for us that we have life, and that more abundantly. Your spirit is in alignment with God's Word by choosing to think on whatsoever things are lovely and of good report.

The Word says that we overcome by the blood of the Lamb and by the word of our testimony. By lining ourselves up with the Word of God, we accept that the debt has been paid by Jesus' stripes. We are therefore conquerors and overcomers wherever we go, wherever our feet tread on this Earth plane. This is the promise that God gave to us as believers and heirs of the Abrahamic covenant.

You are paralleling Jesus' steps. As Jesus took the Word to the low places, the hellish places, you are doing likewise and demonstrating, as Jesus did, that he is Lord over heaven and Earth. Jesus said as he destroyed yokes, did miracles, signs and wonders, we likewise would do the same and *would do greater things*. Jesus preached to thousands, but in this modern age, it is possible to reach millions at any one given moment in time. The technology is growing so fast that it may soon be possible to reach billions.

When you overcome, your past imprisonment now becomes a testimony of God's goodness. Your life, like Joseph's will then become a living epistle of God's greatness, majesty and dominion of the Earth. The Word says that after you have suffered a while, He will exalt you. As Jesus emerged from the tomb, it is just a matter of time before your day will come and you will go before the king, the warden, your supervisor, past enemies, or your doctor, and receive your promotion, your release, restored relationships, or your clean bill of health.

The caveat is that we first must demonstrate mastery over the negative forces in our life. Jesus told the disciples that if they wanted to reign with Him in glory, they must be followers of Christ (Mark 10:35-45). Jesus practiced forgiveness. He did not seek to revenge his enemies, but rather to love and serve them. Jesus did not dismay and say look at how many thousands had been blessed because of him, but was instead obedient to the cross. Neither did Jesus look for someone to take him down from the cross.

Stop looking for someone to rescue you. Once you have gained mastery over the negative forces in your life, the doubts, the fears, the disbelief, the sense of unworthiness, you are then able to put yourself in the pool, rather than waiting for someone else to do it. *It is then that we are able to take title back and possess the land, the houses, the businesses, the relationships, our health etc.*

Instead of revenge, Joseph practiced forgiveness, obedience to God's Word, long suffering, patience, faith, and he continued to serve God. Like Jesus and Esther, he prayed, remained optimistic and gave God praise in spite of his circumstances. Joseph was eventually rescued by his own gifts as opposed to the direct efforts of the chief cupbearer he had helped. Joseph's gift made room for him and brought him before the Pharaoh and other great men. Joseph possessed the title deed, [*the internal robe of righteousness*]. It was a just a matter of time before he could come forth and claim what was rightfully his, according to the Abrahamic covenant.

When you follow in Joseph's footsteps, it is then that you will have a testimony, a plan, to empower others to be set free from their bondage. When you have accomplished this, then it is now time for your curtain call. Luke 21:28 tells us to, "…lift up your heads; for your redemption draweth nigh."

Step 9
Success and the Paparazzi

> Then Pharaoh sent and called Joseph, and they brought him hastily out of the dungeon: and he shaved himself, and changed his raiment, and came in unto Pharaoh... And Pharaoh said unto Joseph, Forasmuch as God hath shewed thee all this, there is none so discreet and wise as thou art: Thou shall be over my house, and according unto thy word shall all my people be ruled...I have set thee over all the land of Egypt.
>
> Genesis 41:14-41

We must position ourselves like Joseph in a state of readiness so that when it is time for our release or promotion, we can step forward quickly and take possession of the land, the job, the relationship, etc. We must be ever vigilant and always prepared to get the call from the warden, the parole board, the governor, the supervisor, the director, or whoever is in a position of authority that can launch us to the next level. The Bible tells us to occupy until Christ comes, to be in a state of readiness so that we can go to the next level. The question arises as to how we occupy in the natural and the spirit realm until we get our curtain call.

If we look at Joseph, we see that during his prison experience, he positioned himself by excelling in everything he touched. He was an ideal prisoner and a role model to the other prisoners. He was well read and knowledgeable about the world and how to interact with people. He stayed abreast of current events. The Bible tells us that he was handsome and well built. We conclude from this that he exercised and took care of his body. In order to have an athletic build, he had to eat foods that were not fatty and loaded with sweets and empty nourishment.

Joseph's mind was keen, and he was well versed in the systems of commerce and world trade. He was able to instantly give the Pharaoh a plan as to how to save not only Egypt, but all nations from famine as well. Joseph was knowledgeable about the environment, and how to preserve food and livestock. Like the good wife in Proverbs 31, he bought the livestock of the inhabitants of Egypt and Canaan for the Pharaoh. When their livestock was gone, Joseph bought their land, and finally without any resources remaining, they offered themselves as slaves. He then gave them seed so that they could farm the land, and imposed a tax system as law that forced them to give the Pharaoh one fifth of its yield. Only the land of the priests did not become the Pharaoh's.

Joseph was a good administrator and knew how to delegate authority to others. He knew how to choose men who were trustworthy, hard workers, able and willing to follow directions. Joseph commanded men under him to set up a system of storing food, and he also kept records. Eventually, Joseph stopped keeping records because its yield was beyond measure.

Joseph did not seek the lights and acclaim of men. He was satisfied to do it God's way. Joseph shared the stage with others by passing on his knowledge, and empowering other like-minded individuals to hold positions of authority and carry out his master plan of the redemption of mankind from famine. His actions paralleled and were a dress rehearsal of sorts for Jesus' spiritual plan of redemption for mankind.

Like the Proverbs 31 woman, Joseph helped the poor. He was also a manufacturer, importer, manager, farmer, merchant, and businessman that was able to pass on generational wealth and a livelihood to his children. Joseph also, like the Proverbs 31 woman, was not only known all around town, but also all around the world, and was admired by all.

Joseph named his children in remembrance of his ordeals and victories so that their names would be living testimonies of God's goodness, and would leave a spiritual legacy for generations yet unborn. Every time the name of his son Manasseh was spoken, his heirs would know that "God has made me forget all my trouble and all my father's household." When the name of his son Ephraim was spoken, the listener would know by interpretation that "God has made me fruitful in the land of my suffering."

Joseph cleaned himself up and changed his clothes when he went before the Pharaoh, so that he was acceptable and credible to those in positions of power and authority. In the secular world, when prisoners are released from jail, they give them new clothes so that they will fit into society. Likewise, we must go shopping for new clothes and new friends, and we must clean up our old image so that people won't reject us because of our prison experience.

We must take a personal inventory as to how we present ourselves to others. An honest response to the following eight questions would help us change our self image and make ourselves presentable to those in authority: 1) Does our outward robe need to be changed? 2) Is there anything about us that makes us stand out like a sore thumb? 3) Do we dress like we are still in bondage? 4) What about our speech - do we have command of the King's language? 5) Do we need to lose weight, fix our teeth, or look more attractive? 6) Do we still look or sound like our prison buddies with their sad, defeatist, negative attitudes? 7) Do we give off a bodily stench that smells like our past? 8) Do we give others the opportunity to reject us before we even open our mouths?

Joseph's self image was intact and he did not bring any emotional baggage [prison mindset, victim mentality] with him to his interview with the Pharaoh. Joseph had changed his clothes [his mindset], he didn't attempt to explain that he was unjustly imprisoned. Joseph respected authority, answered questions posed to him in a brilliant manner, and stayed focused. He did not take credit for his gift, instead he gave honor to God as being the source of his gift, wisdom, talents and brilliance.

Joseph was not awe-struck either by talking to someone in authority, like the Pharaoh. Joseph had communed daily with the Creator of the universe and knew of God's mighty acts and nature. Joseph's desire was to gain the applause of God and not man. Joseph's quest was to hear God say, "Well done, thou good and faithful servant!" Joseph knew at the core of his being that if God was for him, the creator of the universe, no one could be against him. Joseph was respectful towards the Pharaoh, but in awe of God only.

Joseph acted as if he was already the head, God's appointed man to do the task, before the Pharaoh could ask him. He did so by volunteering a plan to save Egypt and the world from famine. Like Jesus, the government was put upon Joseph's shoulders.

Joseph did not attempt to hobnob, play games, and look for opportunities to be promoted. God promoted Joseph - plain and simple. The government was at Joseph's beck and call. Joseph became a mighty counselor and prince of peace, like Jesus. Joseph followed the Word that says, "Seek ye first the kingdom of God, and all things shall be added," and was consequently promoted as the head.

If we want to get to the palace like Joseph did, we must be in a state of readiness. We must learn how to occupy until our day in court comes, or until we are called for that important interview that will launch us to the next level. We must first mentally visualize while we are in prison that we have already arrived. We claim that next blessing by becoming it already. Like a consummate runner, we must visualize ourselves crossing the finish line in our mind.

Once we see it in our mind, we must become it! If we want to become a world champion golfer, then we must like Tiger Woods practice and play golf every day. Like Tiger, bring along your coach and support system with you if possible. No man is a success by himself. Seek out and train individuals that believe in your dream. Get away from the naysayers that say you will always be depressed, addicted, poor, in prison, the projects, the ghetto, a mental institution, or that you will always be the *tail* and not the *head.*

See yourself on that interview explaining like Joseph, how if necessary you can function as a troubleshooter, and come up with solutions where there is no answer. Don't go into the interview speaking in tongues, attempting to be super spiritual. Let the Christ in you speak for itself by your successful track record while in prison, or while on difficult assignments on previous jobs. Let the employer know that you have the answers, that you have knowledge and skills that will empower his company to grow, and that you are *willing to submit to his authority*. If asked what your source of inspiration is, then by all means acknowledge God as the source.

If your gift is in the area of writing, then show the editor your manuscript or book. If it is in singing, then bring your demo tape. Whatever your field of expertise is, bring your portfolio so that the interviewer can see what you have done. Bring the fruit of your prison experience with you to the next level, and began to market and sell it. Put the systems in writing and leave a blueprint of success, so that others will be empowered to prosper and overcome their prison experiences.

Don't look for the lights to find you, and don't hog them when they shine on you. Express your gift even if the lights don't shine on you. If your anointing is to play the piano, then do it even if you are not recognized. It your manuscript is turned down, publish it yourself. If your anointing is to bake desserts, than give away samples like Famous Amos did, until you are discovered. Whatever your talent, gift, or specialty is, do it because you love doing it when no one is watching, and success will find you.

Remember that Joseph was brought "hastily out of prison." Because Joseph was prepared in all respects, he could execute a plan of salvation instantly that was readily acceptable to the Pharaoh. We, as believers, must position ourselves like Joseph so that we can respond immediately and convincingly to our supervisors, and leave them with no doubts that we can get the job done.

Let your value be such that *they will hunt you down* like the paparazzi chases Britney Spears. Don't forget to bring along the gleaners, those who believe in your dream, and elevate them accordingly. Delegate responsibility to them so that your vision can expand and reach the masses long after you have left this earthly plane. Leave a legacy and the title deed like Abraham did for generations yet unborn that share your biological as well as spiritual DNA.

Step 10
Celebrating Your Victories

And Pharaoh took off his ring from his hand, and put it upon Joseph's hand, and arrayed him in vestures of fine linen, and put a gold chain about his neck; And he made him to ride in the second chariot which he had; and they cried before him, Bow the knee: and he made him ruler over all the land of Egypt.

Genesis 41:42-43

There are some experiences in life that are so painful that when we transcend them, we are left in a numb-like position. It is as if we stand there frozen, waiting for the next wave to come inland and swallow us up, just like Hurricane Katrina overtook New Orleans. This is when it is important to have friends, someone from the outside that can validate your experience and tell you that - the storm is over, you survived it, you are not crazy, and congratulate you on your accomplishments. It is important that you mark the occasion by going shopping, dancing or letting your hair down in some fashion.

That's what the Pharaoh did for Joseph; he drew a line in the sand and announced that it was a new day for Joseph. He marked it by giving him a ring on his finger and vestures of fine linen that announced his adoption into the royal family. Joseph's dream of headship had finally come true at the age of 30, after spending 11 years as a slave and over two years in prison. The government was now upon Joseph's shoulders. William Cullen Bryant was right when he said that, "truth crushed to earth, shall rise again." Joseph had been to the pit of hell, had survived the test, and it was now the appointed time of his redemption and resurrection.

We glory in the blessings and the favor that was given to him by the Pharaoh, but do we realize that they are a reflection of what God has in store for us in this life, and in the life hereafter? God tells us to consider how the lilies are arrayed [robed] to demonstrate the superiority of God's blessings in comparison to what earthly fathers who are of a sinful nature can give us.

God's promise is to array [robe] those that love Him with goodness and mercy. He says that it will follow us all the days of our life. When the floods come, His promise is that it will not come near us. His promise is that we will be spared from the famine and enjoy the abundant life. God's love is such that He tells us that a thousand may fall at our right hand, but it shall not come near to us. God's promise is to set before us an open door that no man can shut.

God prepares a table of blessings before us in the presence of our enemies. His promise is to give his angels charge over us, to keep us from all harm and danger (Psalm 91:11). He anoints our head [our understanding] with oil [the Holy Spirit] so that we will have the strength to overcome our enemies. And when we have endured the race like Joseph did, we will receive a new robe of righteousness, and our cup will overflow with goodness and mercy, and we will dwell in the consciousness [house] of the Lord, which is peace, joy, and love, forever. This promise is not just for us to experience here on Earth, but also for life eternal.

His brothers could not strip Joseph of his new Egyptian robe. Joseph could not be tried twice or be a victim of double jeopardy. They could not even get near Joseph without Joseph's or his guards' permission. Joseph had a hedge of protection around him. But more importantly, they could not strip him of his internal robe of righteousness and favor with God.

Joseph's array in the natural was a metaphor for what God did for Joseph in the spirit realm. The Word says in the secret place, we were physically formed. Likewise, in the spirit realm, in the secret place, in that dark prison, Joseph was refined, reborn with a robe of righteousness. Joseph received a new and superior anointing [vestures of fine linen] that made him the *head* and not the *tail*. Joseph also took possession of the land and inherited the wealth of his adversaries.

Once Joseph was recreated in the secret place, God then rewarded him openly so that all men could see the mysterious and marvelous works of God. Who but God can take a dead, forsaken, imprisoned thing and breathe life, wholeness, and joy back into it? Only God has the power to resurrect the dead. Only God can take a caterpillar and transform it into a butterfly! It was now time for Joseph to celebrate his release.

I experienced a major breakthrough in 2007 during a national real estate famine in sales and an explosion in foreclosures nation-wide.[29] The Chicago Sun-Times published an article on November 14, 2007 that reported the following:

> Sales of existing homes in the U.S. are forecast to decline to a five-year low in 2007, a trade group for real estate agents said Tuesday, and the outlook for 2008 is worsening. The ninth-straight downwardly revised monthly forecast from the National Association of Realtors calls for U.S. existing home sales to fall 12.7 percent this year to 5.66 million, the lowest level since 2002.[30]

After 24 years in real estate, I was shocked by the brutal assault the market had on homeowners, property owners, and ancillary services that feed off of the real estate industry. I too, like many brokers chose to downsize and cut expenses. My husband and I decided to sell or lease a commercial building we owned so that we could pay off our mounting debts since sales were declining. God was faithful, and we sold the property after it had been on the market for over 10 months for *more than 4 times what we paid for it*. Indeed, this became a new day for us and *enabled us to pay off all of our debts,* except for good debt on properties that are appreciating in value while we write off the mortgage interest.

God is not a respecter of person, and when your time of release comes make sure you take time to mark the day by throwing yourself a party. It is important that you realize the storm is over. It is tempting to try to position yourself for another storm, because the onslaught of the past storm is so deadly that you think that another Tsunami will overtake you at any moment. You may still feel awkward and shell shocked; but that is natural. You must give yourself time to adjust to your new clothes, new friends, new anointing and new environment.

Know that it is okay, that God has not let you survive the lion

---

[29] http://www.mortgagebankers.org/NewsandMedia/PressCenter/50974.htm

[30] http://www.suntimes.com/business/648842,CST-FIN-1bit14.article

and the giant only to be overtaken by another monster. God's will is that we have life, and that more abundantly. Know that God has something greater in store for you to claim. Yes, other devils will come with this new level, but the same God that enabled you to overcome the lion and the giant will give you the victory over your enemies outside, and your inner me's. God's will for us is that we go from victory to victory, from glory to glory. God is faithful! Remember, He sent his only Son that we might have life, and that more abundantly.

So bring out the fatted calf, go shopping, and name your place of redemption "Bethel," because it was there that God revealed himself to you and showed himself strong. Teach your biological and spiritual children about your Bethel experiences. Write it down in their hearts and if possible, put it in writing so that you and they will have a living memorial of God's goodness.

Step 11
Releasing the Pain of the Past

And Joseph called the name of the firstborn Manasseh: For God, said he, hath made me forget all my toil, and all my father's house. And the name of the second called he Ephraim: For God hath caused me to be fruitful in the land of my affliction.

Genesis 41:51-52

Joseph did not dwell on the past - he got over it and forgave his brothers. The proof that he accepted his past was evident in that he could name his children in remembrance of what he had overcome. When you forget those things that lie behind, and press towards the high calling, you can then give birth to a Manasseh and an Ephraim. Joseph named his first child, Manasseh, which translates, "God has made me to forget all my trouble and all my father's household." His second child was named, Ephraim, which means, "God has made me fruitful in the land of my suffering."

Since the beginning of time, some individuals or groups have been deeply wounded, discriminated against, abused, and taken advantage of for various reasons. Sometimes, it can be physical or sexual abuse by a loved one, parent, or someone close to you in a position of trust or authority. It can be an institutionalized social system that keeps one in bondage because of one's robe of color, or being born into a certain caste system, as in India. One's robe of religious beliefs can also cause individuals to lose their lives, or suffer affliction, discrimination, or poverty, as in Ireland or the Middle East.

There are some things we experience in life that are so painful that only God can give us the grace to forget the suffering associated with the event(s). Joseph's brothers, upon realizing that they had reaped what they had sown, said, "…Surely, we are being punished because of our brother. We saw how distressed he [Joseph] was when he pleaded with us for his life, but we would not listen..." (Genesis 42:21 NIV).

What is interesting is that Joseph's brothers believed that

they were receiving recompense for their misdeeds under the Old Testament system of an eye for an eye theology. But instead, and this is one of the reasons why Joseph is a precursor to Jesus Christ, is that Joseph chose to act like Christ would, and forgave his brothers instead of retaliating.

Like Joseph and Jesus, we must take our painful, troubling experiences to God. For He alone can do what is humanly impossible to do. How can we forgive a Hitler, an Ide Amin, a Jeffrey Dalmer, slave masters, rapists, molesters, Sadam Hussein, and others, except if we do it through God's grace? The pain and horror is too great, it is unconscionable to even think about certain crimes that have been committed, let alone forgive the perpetrators.

Once we turn it over to God, however, then we, like Joseph, can name our second born Ephraim, and God can then make us fruitful in the land of our suffering. The key is to first give birth to a Manasseh, so that we can forgive our enemies and let the past be the past. Releasing our enemies frees us up to realize that what the enemy meant for evil, God will use for good. We are then free to take our lemons and make lemonade out of them! We are free to live out and write our story of overcoming so that others who are disenfranchised and disrobed because of abuse, poverty, race, low self-esteem, class, or religion can be set free.

We can then join the ranks of the heroes in Hebrews 11, who suffered persecution for the gospel's sake. Their weakness was turned to strength: and through faith they overcame their enemies. Hebrews 12:12-13 NIV explains it as follows:

> Therefore, strengthen your feeble arms and weak knees. 'Make level paths for your feet', so that the lame may not be disabled, but rather healed.

Like the heroes of faith, we must embrace our weaknesses and not run from them or cover them up. Too many individuals want to conceal their weaknesses in a bottle of alcohol, physically strike back, use street or prescription drugs, sex, or have illicit affairs. We must learn to run like David did to meet our Goliath, knowing and trusting that the battle is not ours, it is the Lord's. We must learn to stand on the Word that says: greater is He that is within us, than he that is in the world; we are more than conquerors through Christ Jesus; if God be for me, who can be against me?

Like Joseph, we must come to the realization that our suffering is not necessarily about us, but about giving birth, and setting free those who are lame and are bruised by society's woes. It takes spiritual maturity to get to this point. We are so inundated with the world's definition of what life is about and what we should pursue in life, we often fall victim to what the media tells us about ourselves, our destiny, and our purpose in life.

We sometimes leave ourselves open to individuals who make their living off of keeping a race or group of people in bondage by continuing to bring up the past. Knowingly or unknowingly, these individuals parade themselves as being leaders, who on the surface masquerade as caretakers of the torch of freedom for disenfranchised individuals or groups. Supposedly, their mission is to help the downtrodden and the "have-nots." They may, however, do some good and bring about some changes, but they also harm these bruised individuals when and if they teach them to keep picking at their wounds.

As a consequence, the wounds are never forgotten and they don't heal. We must remember the past and learn from it, but we have to stop nursing and rehearsing the past. Until we forgive our perpetrators, learn from the experience, and let our wounds become scars, we cannot become fruitful in the land of our suffering, like Joseph did in his. We may have the outward trappings of success, but that sense of shalom will not dwell within us. There will always be something hidden within our psyche, emotions and soul that gives us a sense that something is missing, and something is still broken.

The Bible says to be thankful when God disciplines you. It says in Hebrews 12:10-11 NIV, "...but God disciplines us for our good that we may share in his holiness. No discipline seems pleasant at the time, but painful. Later on, however, it produces a harvest of righteousness and peace for those who have been trained by it." There are some that would argue and say, "What does God have to do with it? Why didn't He stop the perpetrator from harming me or my ancestors?"

I don't have the answers to these questions, and I agree that it seems unfair and cruel what man has done to mankind. But I do know that the Word says the Earth is the Lord's and the fullness thereof. I do know that God said that Jesus came that we might have life, and that more abundantly. God loves mankind so much that He has given man freewill. Unfortunately, with that freewill is the ability to kill, steal, and destroy. And most importantly, I know that the Word says that God disciplines those he loves. There are times, however, for whatever reason, God does not intervene.

In the face of tragedy and unfairness, I can only lean on the Word that was written by individuals inspired by God. The Word tells me that for his followers, what the enemy meant for evil, God will make it good. It further tells me that by enduring the experience and not rendering evil for evil, out of this situation discipline will come. Both discipline and redemption were exemplified in the lives of Joseph, Jesus, Mahatma Gandhi and Reverend Dr. Martin Luther King Jr. The Word further states that later on, however, it produces a harvest of righteousness and peace (Hebrews 12:11 NIV). As stated earlier, the word "peace" in Hebrew means shalom - nothing missing and nothing broken.

Who can argue and say they don't want shalom in their life? Ask the millionaire that is undergoing chemotherapy whether he would prefer a sense of shalom or another million dollars. Anna Nicole Smith's premature death should have made it clear to everyone that there is definitely more to life than money, fame, and sexy looks. Rich or poor, we all long for a sense of well being in our lives and relationships. Without it, money, sex, food, clothing, and houses are all idle trophies. They sit on the shelf, but they can't comfort us or give us peace.

Learn from Joseph, - accept and acknowledge your painful past and dysfunctional behavior. You must come out of denial! Denying your past is denying yourself from enjoying a future free of pain, hurt and depression. Stop beating yourself up by nursing and rehearsing the past. If you consciously or unconsciously played a role in it, ask God for the strength to forgive yourself as well as your perpetrators. Know that after you have endured the test, God will make you fruitful in the land of your suffering and give you inner and outer peace. This is true shalom that money, sex, drugs, friends, or even loved ones can't give you.

Step 12
Staying Calm in the Storm

And he turned himself about from them, and wept; and returned to them again, and communed with them… (Genesis 42:24) And Joseph made haste; for his bowels did yearn upon his brother: and he sought where to weep; and he entered into his chamber, and wept there.

Genesis 43:30

Don't let your enemies see you weep. When relatives and individuals that have hurt you in the past resurface in your life, their presence can be painful, and deeply move you to tears. Set aside a private room, like Joseph did, where you can weep and work through your feelings. After you are done grieving, wash your face and put on some make-up to hide your tears. If you are unable to overcome these past hurts on your own, you must ask God for help in controlling your emotions when you have to commune with these individuals. If you need the services of a professional counselor, then by all means avail yourself of their services [please note that resources are provided in the Appendix of this book]. Don't be ashamed or reluctant to express your humanity. Remember that Jesus wept.

Don't do your grieving in public. Trying to grieve and reconcile your differences with your abusers openly is like picking at a wound that is trying to form a scab. Airing your differences in a Jerry Springer type arena will not bring about healing and reconciliation. Your goal is not to excite your enemy to violence, aggression, or faultfinding, but to bring about peace and harmony.

Your objective is to make it clear to them and others that you have survived, and that you are an overcomer. Like Joseph, we want to be able to say with conviction, "But as for you, ye thought evil against me; but God meant it unto good, to bring to pass, as it is this day, to save much people alive." (Genesis 50:20) These words also echo the sentiments of Jesus while on the cross, in regard to his accusers when he said, "Father, forgive them, for they know not what they do."

It takes spiritual maturity and wisdom to understand that these are battles over spiritual turf. In the movie, Gone With The Wind, at the height of despair, Scarlett O'Hara gets a glimmer of hope when she hears her father's words- "*Land is the only thing that matters,*" reverberate in her spirit. Likewise, in the spirit realm, underneath all the dysfunction in human relationships is a battle over the seed that will inherit *the Earth.* Which will prevail, the seed of Adam [carnal man] or the seed of Abraham [spirit man]? We as fellow believers must realize that the battle is not ours; it is the Lord's (II Chronicles 20:15). We must be wise as serpents, but harmless as doves in order to save many souls and to bring forth Abrahamic seed that will *inherit and possess the land* (Matthew 10:16).

You must be careful as to whom you let get close to you. Remember, you are guarding the seed of Abraham within your bosom. Don't feel obligated to give your past abusers or abusive family members a position of trust where they can hurt you again. Give them wheat, but guard your heart. Before you return to your enemies and place your bosom on theirs, put them to the test and see whether it is safe to confide in them. Your enemies of the past when they see your success will want to embrace and bow down to you, for the wheat they can get from you. Use discernment before you open up and trust them. Give yourself time to work through the hurts of your past. Test your enemies [brothers] like Joseph did, by giving them obstacles to overcome.

It is normal to have ambivalent feelings about your family members who have not let go of their dysfunctional behavior. There may be a part of you that yearns for closeness as Joseph did for his brother Benjamin, and another part of you that feels that you must test your family members to see whether they have rid themselves of their deceptive nature. This sharp dichotomy that Joseph experienced is a metaphor for how you may feel towards the individual that was a trusted parent, loved one, friend or someone in a position of authority that betrayed you. Part of you yearns for a restoration of that closeness, and part of you now has discernment and knows that you must be careful as to who you let get close to you.

The mature Joseph was able to make peace with his good brother and bad brothers. In life, people are not all good or all bad, even after they have given their life to Christ. We must learn how to live with the wheat and the tares. One of the problems with living with tares is that by definition, tares resemble wheat. The difference is that tares are "a species of rye-grass, the seeds of which are a strong soporific [hypnotic] poison. It bears the closest resemblance to wheat till the ear appears, and only then the difference is discovered."[31]

Ironically, some victims of abuse at the hands of strangers may experience this same type of ambivalence towards their perpetrator(s). We have heard of news stories about victims that befriend their abusers, and yes, sometimes even married the offender while that person is in jail. Could it be that somehow the victim becomes attached to the offender that showed them some ounce of humanity by not killing them? Is it a combination of the triumphant spirit in man that chooses to pray for and forgive their enemies and show them mercy? Or is it a tare that has cast a soporific poison and has befriended the unsuspecting victim?

Until we are able to accept the dual nature of good and evil forces within mankind, and discern between the true wheat and the tares, we will continue to come up empty and frustrated, forever looking for perfect people, perfect families, or perfect churches. The key is to love and forgive them, guard your heart and grow to a position of discernment and wisdom, just like Joseph did, so that you can live peacefully with your abusers.

Joseph's spiritual maturity was evident when he saw his older brothers, recognized them as enemies of the past, but had enough sense to keep quiet and not reveal himself. Don't expect your family or your former enemies to embrace or bow down to you because you are now at the top. Don't be surprised if they still see you as their little sister or brother, or the one that got picked on all the time. Remember, Jesus was questioned as to whether any good could come out of Nazareth, and he had to leave his hometown in order to perform miracles.

---

[31] http://dictionary.reference.com/cite.html?qh=tares&ia=easton

There is something about success that is undeniable, however. There will come a point when your enemies will have to bow down and admit that you are the *head.* It may eventually come when they see you in a magazine, or on television, or hear you on the radio. This is when the scars of the past may try to resurrect themselves and wreak havoc in your life.

The pain that surfaces can be so great as you reflect on the past, you will question whether you have truly gotten over those past hurts. There is an internal battle that goes on where you ask yourself, "Didn't I forget the past? After all, I named my firstborn Manasseh because God made me forget all my trouble, and my entire father's household." You will look around at all your possessions, your fame and accomplishments that represent your second son, Ephraim, and realize that in spite of your prosperity, there is still an aching in your heart.

The true test comes, however, when you see your enemies face to face. It is one thing to name it and claim it, but when you spend time with your enemies, any unresolved feelings will undoubtedly bubble to the surface. That is what Joseph faced, and why he had to flee to a private place where he could nurse his scars. Sometimes, it is only when you are in your secret place; under the shadow of the wings of the most high that God can take your scars and completely erase the pain from your conscious and unconscious mind.

It is only Jesus that can take away certain painful memories, to the extent that you don't even have dreams about the past. He alone can wipe your mental and emotional slate clean, and dissolve your scars into smiles. It is Jesus that gives us the ability to forget our troubles, and our father's household. It is only Jesus that can empower a Ruth or an Abraham to leave their homeland and their suffering, and embrace a new family, a new way of life.

Psychotherapy, group counseling, individual counseling, and sometimes medicine can help individuals that have been deeply bruised and traumatized in life. But there is nothing like Jesus' balm of Gilead that can completely heal, set you free and give you spiritual discernment. Jesus is the only one that can make you a new creature (Rev. 21:5). He is the only one that can separate soul and marrow (Hebs. 4:12). Jesus is the only one who has the authority to calm the winds and command the storms in your life to be still.

Again, this emancipation comes only from patiently spending time with Him in your secret place. This is not something that man can give you. It is only when you go apart, and earnestly and diligently seek Him, that will you find Him. This is not something you get on a weekend retreat, or from reading an inspirational book, although both are helpful. Again, it comes from spending time alone with, and communing with Him, listening to his still small voice, not telling Him what you want Him to know or give to you, but listening to him.

It comes down to trusting and believing in His Word. He tells us that without faith, it is impossible to please Him. His will is that we have life, and that more abundantly. His promise is to dry every tear. His promise is to give us the oil of gladness for our mourning. So, take your burdens to the Lord in your secret chamber, and leave them there. Make the exchange with Him like Joseph did, so that you can be that new creature and experience shalom, joy, and tranquility every day, in spite of your circumstances.

Step 13
Reconciliation

And he [Joseph] wept aloud: and the Egyptians and the house of Pharaoh heard (Genesis 45:2)....and as they were leaving he said to them, 'Don't quarrel on the way!'

Genesis 45:24 NIV

There may come a time when you are exposed and your peers, associates, or the media hears of, or delves into your debasing and embarrassing past that still causes you pain, though you are physically and emotionally far removed from it. Your past perpetrators may show up on your doorstep, like Joseph's brothers, did asking for wheat [provisions], once they hear of your accomplishments or fame. You must be prepared for the likelihood of this happening. It is important not to see this as a negative, and attempt to hide from, or cover up your past. This event, if properly handled, can be a healthy step towards reconciling the past for all parties involved.

Although Joseph had forgiven his brothers, the process of reconciliation was not automatic for them. Reconciliation and repentance may take months or years for your abusers or enemies. Or it may never come. Don't expect that when you become the *head*, that your enemies will be able to disengage themselves from their dysfunctional, pathological behavior. Even though Joseph had forgiven them, and had given them abundant provisions, his brothers had not forgiven themselves.

Their guilt and unresolved issues surfaced after the death of their father, Israel, and they feared that Joseph would seek revenge and mistreat them. It was at this point that they finally asked for forgiveness and offered themselves as slaves (Genesis 50:17-18). Their unresolved guilt and fears were so great that they forced Joseph to deal with his past familial issues openly. Although Joseph had already forgiven them, he did so again with the explanation that he understood that their actions were meant for evil, but God allowed his enslavement for the good of mankind, "to save many people alive." True to his word, Joseph did not seek revenge, but took care of them and their descendants (Genesis 50:21).

Climbing this 13th step to *get to the palace* is sometimes obfuscated by the many months or years of our persevering in our wilderness experiences. Although we have survived in our career, marriage, health, or relationships, and have achieved a measure of success, we have not hit jackpot; we haven't entered the Promised Land yet. Often, we don't know how close we are to stepping into the Promised Land, because we are so used to just surviving, but we really aren't "thriving." Our needs are met - we have food, clothing, and shelter, but we are still not in the palace. Others may look at us and feel that we have it made - a nice house, car, spouse, children, job, etc. But in our hearts, we still don't feel that we have arrived.

Something still remains unresolved. In Joseph's case, his brothers had not worked out their guilt feelings towards him. This can be an imposition on the victimized person, because oftentimes, the victimizer's self-perception is that they have been mistreated and they need help. This was seen with the Prodigal's Son's brother. The brother felt victimized and mistreated, taken for granted by their father. The brother was finally set free when the father acknowledged to him that everything that the father had was already his, he simply had to ask for it, like the Prodigal Son.

Each person must define individually what his or her palace experience is. For one individual, it may mean wholesome relationships or marriage to a loving and caring partner. To another person, it may mean a six or seven figure income. To another, it may mean having healthy children. One's palace experience may be literally getting out of jail, and to another person, it may mean getting out of a certain neighborhood, overcoming a physical or addictive condition, or a negative mindset.

The generic definition I choose to use to explain one's palace experience is that of "shalom." This is the benchmark of success that is applicable to any person or situation. Joseph experienced a partial sense of shalom when all his family was reunited in Goshen. But his true sense of shalom did not come until his brothers asked him for forgiveness after the death of their father, and offered themselves as slaves.

The Prodigal Son experienced shalom when he realized that it was better to be a servant in his father's house, than to continue to sow his oats and waste his life and inheritance. His envious brother experienced shalom when he felt loved and validated by his father and accepted not because of what he did, but because of who he was, the son of his father.

Again, as difficult or as unfair as it may seem, the work of reconciliation may primarily fall in the lap of the victimized individual. When you become the *head*, help your enemies to release the past and their dysfunctional behavior. Don't seek to revenge your enemies, but rather, find ways to bless them. As you reconcile your differences and make peace with your enemies, return evil with good. Go beyond what is expected when they ask for provisions. Become what Bruce Wilkinson calls in his book, *The Prayer of Jabez,* "a gimper for God." This disables your enemies and leaves them powerless. It forces them to look to God when they see the resultant miracles in your life.

Show your humanity and your hurt when appropriate, but make peace with your brothers [enemies of the past] privately. Get rid of the unbelievers who don't believe that God allowed this evil for good in order to save many people alive. Not only for the house of Israel, but all mankind. Joseph understood God's will, and that it was not just about Joseph and his hurt feelings. Likewise, as Christian soldiers, we must realize that the battle is not necessarily about us, but the seed of Abraham. Neither is this our battle, it is the Lord's. He will fight it, vindicate us, and give us the victory.

Although Joseph had achieved a victory of sorts by his brothers asking for forgiveness and offering themselves as slaves, he still had to contend with their dysfunctional, quarrelsome personalities. Until your enemies overcome their deficiencies, it is important to remember that they must come up to your level. Forgiveness does not mean that their vile behavior or personalities are eradicated. Their presence and personalities may be a bone of contention, a thorn in the flesh until they change. It is important to arm yourself spiritually and remember your role as an ambassador of sorts, a conduit to bring them to Christ.

As an ambassador to your family, your role may start off as that of a Ruth [truth seeker]. As you evolve spiritually, you may have to literally leave your family, your origins, and cleave to a Naomi and/or a Mordecai [mentors], who know and can keep your compass, i.e. your heart, pointed in the direction of spiritual truths, and teach you how to shoot your victory arrows. In order to break generational curses of immorality, hatred, poverty, addictions, depression, and other "isms," you may have to be the leader, the Moses or the Joseph, that is chosen so that family members, friends, business or social contacts that are steeped in pathological behavior can be set free. This is an awesome task to fill, and you may feel unqualified for the roles assigned to you. But you must remember that the battle is not yours, it is the Lord's. Greater is He that is within you than he that is within the world.

As you continue to search for spiritual truths and obey God's Word, it will definitely cost you something when you are promoted to headship and take on the role of a Joseph. If there is no pain, then there is no gain. Remember, you have a friend in Jesus, and He is well able to heal, comfort, strengthen, and keep you in perfect peace as long as your mind is stayed on Him (Isaiah 26:3).

You may feel strange in the role of a Joseph to your family and peers, but who knows the family and company secrets and pathology better than you. The wheat and the tares must grow up together. Ishmael and Isaac grew up together, and ultimately, our redemption and shalom- and that of the world's-, lie in their seeds being able to live together peacefully, and not separately. Those that know the Word must be conduits for non-believers and save them from the hand of the accuser of the brethren who comes to kill, steal, and destroy (John 10:10).

We live in a world today where spiritual wickedness abounds in high places. It is not just in dysfunctional families, but also in government, law, and politics, and also in the church. You see, wherever there is a body, the enemy seeks to occupy it. I Peter 5:8 says that the enemy like a roaring lion walks about, seeking whom he may devour.

As Joseph lived among his brothers, we must become comfortable living with our abusers or enemies. Living in a monastery is not the answer. We must be like Jesus and make our bed among the have-nots, the lost sheep, the prostitutes, the lonely, the spiritually wicked ones in high places, as well as the bruised and broken hearted. We must be willing to touch the modern day lepers, the "untouchables" of society - those in cancer and AIDS wards, ghettos, nursing homes and homeless shelters.

Living among our abusers or enemies is not easy, but if we want to experience shalom, we must daily practice forgiveness, and keep ourselves spiritually charged and renewed. Once we disarm our enemies by forgiving them, and master living with them, we can then take the final step found in the next chapter and enter the Promised Land, that place of shalom in mind, body and spirit.

Step 14
Maintaining a Spirit of Shalom

> And Joseph made ready his chariot, and went up to meet Israel his father, to Goshen, and presented himself unto him; and he fell on his neck, and wept on his neck a good while.
>
> Genesis 46:29

There is so much to this last step, it is hard to know where to begin. Although this step is the end, it is also the beginning of a new life - free from weeping, persecution, doubting, discouragement, and pain. It is the climax of God's promise to believers to dry every tear. It signifies an accomplishment in the natural, but more importantly, it speaks of victory in the world to come. It speaks metaphorically of our reuniting with Christ. It speaks of our making ready our chariot [our heart] to meet the Father in the spirit realm, and to dwell with him here on Earth in heavenly places.

As Joseph went up to meet his father, we wait to go up and meet Jesus, with great anticipation. The angels and the mighty crowd of witnesses also wait to greet and embrace us, we who are the remnant of all tribes and nations of the Earth, we who have washed our robes, [our lives] in the blood of the Lamb. We who have washed our robes by submitting to God's Word, by doing his will, by using the gifts [our robes] that He has given to us for the body of Christ, so that the lame, the broken hearted, the bruised may be healed.

As Joseph wept a long time when he saw his father, I believe we too shall weep a long time when we meet our heavenly Father. Like Joseph, I believe our tears will be tears of gladness. And when Jesus wipes our tears away, they will be gone forever (Revelation 7:9-17). It is the fulfillment of Mark 10:29-30, which reads:

> ...There is no man that hath left house, or brethen, or sisters, or father, or mother, or wife, or children, or lands, for my sake,

> and the gospel's, But he shall receive an *hundred-fold now in this time*, houses and brethen, and sisters, and mothers, and children, and lands, *with persecutions*; and in the world to come eternal life.

After years of imprisonment mentally, emotionally, spiritually and physically, Joseph finally experienced shalom when his brothers asked for forgiveness and were reconciled back to him [metaphorically, the Christ]. In the presence of his enemies [*with persecutions*], God had prepared a table of bounty for Joseph, his family and descendants (Psalms 23:5). Surely, goodness and mercy followed Joseph all the days of his life and his consciousness, his mindset remained in the house of the Lord, in a state of shalom forever (Psalm 23:6).

Joseph embraced his brothers and gave them the best of Egypt as commanded by the Pharaoh: carts loaded with the best provisions, best land, new clothes, and silver. Joseph settled his father and his brothers in Egypt, and gave them property in the best part of the land. They acquired property there and were fruitful and increased greatly in number (Genesis 47:11-27 NIV). We are told in Genesis 47:6 that the Pharaoh gave his descendants jobs befitting their talents and ability. He told Joseph that if he knew of any with special abilities, to put them in charge of his own livestock.

As the famine worsened, the Egyptians eventually sold their land and then themselves as slaves, but the Israelites prospered and greatly increased in numbers (Genesis 47:23-27). Not only did the Israelites prosper in the here and now, but their descendants also received a blessing that is still with them to this day. Jacob's dream in Genesis 28:12-15 wherein God told him that he would make a great nation out of Israel's seed was finally fulfilled.

We too, as Abraham's descendants, must grab hold of the baton of faith, whereby we have been grafted into his lineage and run to our palaces (Romans 11:17 NIV). Our preordained destiny lies there, but we must take the steps of faith as outlined in Joseph's 14-Step Recovery Program.

Like Joseph, we must first determine what our gifts and

dreams are telling us about our future. We must discover what our unique ornamented robe that God has given and designed especially for us is (Step 1). What are the prophecies that have been spoken over our lives? What are our dreams, our early morning awakenings telling us about our preordained destiny (Step 2)? We then must be willing to obey God's Word and endure potentially months or years of mental, physical, financial, or spiritual imprisonment before our dreams manifest (Steps 3-6). There is an expression in the secular world that holds true, and is applicable in the spirit realm, "No pain, no gain!"

Please note that this is typically a generational battle. By this, I mean that it is a battle that may be and often is played out and continued from one generation to the next. One generation may plant the seed, and another may water, and another reaps the increase (I Cor. 3:6-7). Of course, it can be played out in one generation, as we see in Joseph's life. In the cog of life, we must figure out and spiritually discern what our purpose is, and how it intertwines with God's plan for humanity.

The common denominator that binds us together through history is faith. Dr. Martin Luther King Jr. put it this way; "I may not get there with you, but we as a people will get to the Promised Land." He also quoted Bryant and said that, "truth crushed to earth, shall rise again." I believe that Dr. King understood that he was a seed being planted, and that he had to die so that new life- freedom for African Americans, people of color and bruised humanity of whatever color or sex would be set free.

The variables are time, wisdom, understanding, obedience, and God's will. It is God that promotes us according to his grand scheme of things. We may want to get to the palace at a certain time, but God may want us to remain in our prison a little longer. Many times, the reason is not clear why our imprisonment lasts as long as it does.

One reason may be that he wants to purify us, like gold, for a specific assignment that He has for us that will benefit humanity. God, in his wisdom, may see our imprisonment as an opportunity to thresh us like wheat so that He may get at the grain, the seed, and the essence of who we are. It is after we have stood the test that He knows that He can count on us; that come hell or high water, we will not deny Him. I Peter 5:10 NIV says that after we have suffered a while, He will perfect, establish, strengthen, and settle us. His ways are not our ways. Our job is to trust God, when we can't see Him, or feel Him, or when all hell breaks loose and we feel forsaken (Steps 7-8).

There is a difference when God promotes us, and when man promotes us. It is important that we don't confuse the two and think that they are the same. Man may promote us to a job, a political office or some other assignment based on their needs, through the lenses of how they see life or their company's or government's needs. God's promotions are never specific to one individual, they always benefit all humanity, and often times don't make sense to the human mind. God promotes according to his will and gives favor as he sees fits to individuals and groups.

God chose the Jews to express his Son in the flesh because they were a monotheistic people. God does not promote according to pedigree, race, color, sex, or education. He will promote a shepherd boy like David singing to him in the wilderness, or a Paul that attempted to destroy Christianity by persecuting Christians. He promoted Ruth, a poor Moabitess, and Rahab, a Gentile prostitute to be a part of his ancestral lineage. Again, the common denominator for all of these individuals was their faith in one God, Jehovah Jireh that sent his only son to Earth to die on the cross so that all humanity might have a right to the tree of life.

We must remember that it is not always about us when we are going through our fiery furnaces of affliction, persecution, and imprisonment, whether they are imposed on us from others or self-imposed. Oftentimes, God is preparing and strengthening us for a specific task so that someone else will be drawn to Christ from our experiences and our testimony. Paul explained his thorn in the flesh that God would not remove as follows:

> And lest I should be exalted above measure through the abundance of the revelations, there was given to me a thorn in

> the flesh, the messenger of Satan to buffet me, lest I should be exalted above measure. For this thing I besought the Lord thrice, that it might depart from me. And he said unto me, My grace is sufficient for thee; for my strength is made perfect in weakness. Most gladly therefore will I rather glory in my infirmities, that the power of Christ may rest upon me (2 Cor. 12:7-9).

As we obey God's Word, we must be ready to give an account of what God has placed in our hearts. As we strive towards our palace and enjoy our palace experiences, we must continue to grow and maintain a spirit of excellence, love, forgiveness, and compassion. We must continue to hone our skills, talents and gifts so that we can remain in our palace, in the Promised Land.

I think the most important thing to remember is that the palace experience is first and foremost a state of mind. Once we grab hold of it in the mind, wherever we are planted, whether we are abased or esteemed, we will have a spirit of shalom in our minds and hearts. And where the mind is, the body will follow. So if we want to be the *head*, and remain the *head*, we must exercise authority over the mind, and the body can't help but follow.

It is when we are at our wits end, that we are often the closest to our miracle, *our palace experience*. It is said that the darkest hour is just before dawn. When it is our time to go to higher places of authority and heavenly places, we must clean ourselves up and put on our best clothes. We must be prepared to give an account of what we have learned during our time of imprisonment, and show the world a better way to accomplish the task at hand, so that many people will live and enjoy a better life. The Word tells us to, "...strengthen your feeble arms and weak knees. Make level paths for your feet, so that the lame may be not be disabled, but rather healed." (Step 9)

When we arrive at our palace, however we define it, we must like Joseph let the world know that God is the source of our strength. Although this takes the glory away from the individual, it opens the door to all by letting everyone know that they have access to God's love, forgiveness, intelligence, creativity, and strength.

Everyone loves a rags to riches story. Some secular examples of individuals who have been victorious over different forms of imprisonment are Oprah Winfrey and Nelson Mandela. Oprah demonstrated to the world how she overcame sexual abuse and made it possible for many to live a better, and not bitter life. As President of South Africa, Nelson Mandela demonstrated after his release from 27 years of imprisonment how to peacefully begin the process of equality in an apartheid torn country.

By letting the world know that it is God who is the source of your promotion, your palace experience, you open the door to all by letting them know that they have access to the palace as well. Your testimony of God's faithfulness tells them that they are heirs to God's promises, found in Deuteronomy 28:1-14 NIV. It reads as follows:

> If you fully obey the LORD your God and carefully follow all his commands I give you today, the LORD your God will set you high above all the nations on earth... The LORD will make *you the head, not the tail.* If you pay attention to the commands of the LORD your God that I give you this day and carefully follow them, you will always be at the top, never at the bottom. Do not turn aside from any of the commands I give you today, to the right or to the left, following other gods and serving them.

The Bible is our warranty deed that gives us title to the land. It is our ticket that will get us into the palace. In Genesis 13:15, God told Abraham that all the land that he saw would be given to him and his seed forever. This title to the land is not an actual warranty deed per se, but the ability to prosper and to experience shalom. It is a God-given favor; an anointing to succeed at whatever is in our hearts to do that will benefit mankind, and is in line with the will of God, wherever we are on this planet Earth.

It is important that as you achieve new levels of success, you throw yourself a party and celebrate each ascension. This is important especially for "A Type" personalities like Joseph that have the ability to focus on a task despite intense opposition. We must not get so goal minded or heavenly focused that we can't enjoy the ride, and stop to smell the roses (Step 10).

Neither should we deny our feelings and become a martyr or saint. Joseph is remarkable in that he was very manly, but in touch with his feelings of sadness and anger. The difference between him and many of us, and this is what made Joseph great, was that he could express his emotions in a positive life affirming way that brought about redemption and reconciliation with his enemies (Steps 11-13).

In the palace, we must continue to grow and learn all we can about world systems and technology so that our seed will remain in the Promised Land. We must be vigilant and look for gleaners with special abilities that we can partner with, and propel to their destinies (Step 14). We must follow mentors like Bill Gates, who chooses individuals who share his dream, and have talents, skills and a commitment to excellence that empowers him and his employees to be successful.

In Exodus 18:20-22 NIV this same advice was given to Moses from his father-in-law Jethro, [who was not an Israelite] as follows:

> Teach them the decrees and laws, show them the way to live and the duties they are to perform. But select capable men from all the people- men who fear God, trustworthy men who hate dishonest gain- and appoint them as officials over thousands, hundreds, fifties and tens. Have them serve as judges for the people at all times, but have them bring every difficult case to you; the simple cases they can decide themselves. That will make your load lighter, because they will share it with you.

In order to remain rooted and grounded and not get burnt out or discouraged, we must teach others God's Word and delegate authority to trustworthy believers. Neither should we become so consumed with the vision that we neglect our family or ourselves. One of the first safety instructions you receive on an airplane is to put the oxygen mask on yourself before you place your child's mask on. If you lose consciousness or run out of air because you have taken care of everyone else's needs, how will the Word be transmitted to the next generation?

It is important as well that we don't take on a savior

mentality. God wants us to *spread* the Word to all nations, not to be junior gods or spokesmen for God. God's ways are not our ways, and his thoughts are not our thoughts. No man can speak for God; we can only say what He has revealed to us. I Cor 13:12 reads, "For now we see through a glass, darkly; but then face to face: now I know in part; but then shall I know even as also I am known."

We, as believers, are all ministers and we must spread the Word first and foremost by our actions and not necessarily by our words. When we do this and adversity comes to our doors like September 11, a Tsunami, or a Hurricane Katrina, we will know how to seek God for others and ourselves. And when that fateful day eventually comes and it is time to shut our eyelids, we will know that to be absent from the body is to be present with the Lord.

Like a well-trained soldier, we must perform our duties, march in place and know that as we occupy until Jesus returns, generational blessings will flow from our loins. As we take this final step, out of our belly will flow living water that Jesus spoke about to the woman at the well. As we teach our children these truths, and practice them in our lives, we have a whole life insurance policy, a title deed that ensures that our seed will dwell in goodness and mercy from generation to generation, infinitum.

We all must answer the question as to what legacy we are leaving for our genetic and spiritual descendants. Is it a legacy of generational curses – hatred, ignorance, illiteracy, dysfunction, high blood pressure, sickness, marital discord, divorce, single parenthood, greed, or poverty to name a few? Or is it a legacy of generational blessings – love, faith in the God of Abraham, wisdom, health, intact families, wealth, philanthropy, unencumbered real estate, stocks and bonds?

Without a doubt, God does want us to prosper and be in good health (III John 1:2). But if we don't leave a testament of living water, then we have aborted the birth process in our lives. We may have a testament of good health, successful children, houses, real estate, stocks and bonds, but we have won the battle and lost the war. The real war is over *spiritual turf* - who will inherit the Earth and leave *living water* to generations yet unborn. We are told in Deuteronomy 30:19 that God has set before us this day, life and death, blessing and cursing, and we are instructed to choose life so that both we and our seed may live.

My prayer is that this will be our ultimate quest, to taste of the living water that Jesus spoke to the woman at the well about so that our thirst would be satiated. When we have washed our earthly robes and exchanged them for heavenly ones, then we truly have reached *the palace*, that *place of shalom in our hearts, minds and spirit.* We can then go up like Joseph and meet our Father, Jehovah Jireh. And when we have passed on living water to the next generation, our souls can say, like Israel when he saw Joseph, "*Now let me die*, since I have seen thy face, because *thou art yet alive*" (Genesis 46:30).

To the reader, I congratulate you as you strive towards this final step. Enjoy the journey, Godspeed and Stay Blessed!

APPENDIX: Resources

[Note to the reader: Detailed below are National Resources for individuals trying to overcome loneliness, depression, discrimination, barrenness, abuse, and other self-destructive behaviors. This list is by no means exhaustive, but it is an attempt to identify resources found in most major cities across the United States. The author is not affiliated with and does not personally endorse any of these organizations, and is not responsible or liable for any of its services or products.]

RESOURCES AND HELP FOR INDIVIDUALS DEALING WITH LONELINESS, DEPRESSION, RUNAWAYS & MISSING PERSONS	
Counseling Center	www.couns.uiuc.edu/brochures/loneline.htm
Walking-Wounded.Net (Christian based)	www.walking-wounded.net
Self-Help Support Groups for Older Women by Lenard W. Kaye	http://books.google.com/books
Crisis Helpline (for any kind of crisis)	(800) 233-4357
Youth Crisis Hotline	(866) 4-U-TREVOR
Common Ground Sanctuary	(800) 231-1127
Crisis Line for the Handicapped	(888) 711-TEEN
National Child – At Risk Hotline	(800) FOR A CHILD
National Runaway Switchboard	(800) 621-4000
National Youth Crisis Hotline (Christian Based)	(800) 448-4663
Depression/Alcohol and Drug Addiction Hotline	(800) 861-1768
National Hopeline Network (Suicide Prevention)	(800) 784-2433
National Runaway Switchboard	(800) RUNAWAY
Covenant House "Nineline"	(800) 999-9999
National Center for Missing & Exploited Children	(800) 843-5678

National Runaway for the Hearing Impaired	(800) 621-0394 (TDD)
Child Find of America	(800) 426-5678

RESOURCES AND HELP FOR INDIVIDUALS DEALING WITH DISCRIMINATION	
National AIDS Hotline	(800) 342-2437
CDC AIDS Info	(800) 232-4636
The Teen AIDS Hotline	(800) 440-TEEN
National Sexually Transmitted Disease Hotline	(800) 227-8922
AIDS in Prison Project's Hotline	1-718-378-7022
The American with Disabilities Act Information and Assistance	(800) 514-0301
The Gay and Lesbian National Hotline	(888) 843-4564
CDC National Prevention Information Network	(800) 458- 5231
AIDS Info	(800) 448-0440
National Women's Health Resource Center	(877) 986-9472
(NAMI) National Alliance for the Mentally Ill Helpline	(800) 950-6264
Mental Health America	(800) 969-6642
Office for Civil Rights	(800) 368-1019

RESOURCES AND HELP FOR INDIVIDUALS DEALING WITH BARRENNESS, UNDEREMPLOYMENT AND UNEMPLOYMENT	
Planned Parenthood Hotline	(800) 230–7526
The Fertility Institute	(800) 433-9009
American Infertility Association	(888) 917-3777
National Women's Health Information Center	(800) 994-9662
http://www.literacydirectory.org/	(800) 228-8813
http://www.careeronestop.org/	(877) 348-0502
www.getthejob.com	Feedback@getthejob.com
www.superpages.com	(800) 376-0136
www.careerbuilder.com	(866) 438-1485
www.employment.com	Info@employment.com
www.snagajob.com	(877) 461-7624
www.jobfox.com	(888) 667-8080

RESOURCES AND HELP FOR INDIVIDUALS DEALING WITH ADDICTIONS AND COMPULSIVE DISORDERS

Cocaine Anonymous	(800) 347-8998
National Help Line for Substance Abuse	(800) 662-HELP
Drug Abuse Information & Referral Line	(800) 662-4357
AL Anon	(888) 425-2666
Sexual Compulsive Anonymous	(800) 977- HEAL
Sex Addiction Helpline	(866) 464-HEAL
Sexual Addicts Anonymous	(800) 477-8191
Anorexia Nervosa and Associated Disorders	(800) 445-1900
National Eating Disorder Association	(800) 931-2237
Overeater Anonymous	(505) 891-2664
Debtors Anonymous	(781) 453-2743

RESOURCES AND HELP FOR INDIVIDUALS DEALING WITH SEXUAL, DOMESTIC, DRUG, CHEMICAL ABUSE, & OTHER DISORDERS	
National Domestic Violence Hotline	(800) 799-7233
National Child Abuse Hotline	(800) FOR A CHILD
National Child Health Abuse Hotline	(800) 422-4453
National Counsel on Child Abuse & Family Violence	(800) 222-2000
National Herpes Hotline	(800) 232-4636
Rape & Abuse & Incest National Network	(800) 656-HOPE
National Domestic Violence Hotline	(800) 799-7233
Psychiatric and Substance Abuse Hotline	(800) 331-2900
Al-Anon for Families of Alcoholics	(800) 344-2666
Alcohol and Drug Helpline	(800) 821-4357
Families Anonymous	(800) 736-9805
National Council on Alcoholism and Drug Dependence	(800) 622-2255
Be Sober Hotline	(800) 237-6237
1 800 Alcohol Recovery Center	(800) 252-6465
Alcohol & Drug Abuse National Clearing House	(800) 729-6686
The American Anorexia/Bulimia Association	(800) 522-2230
Victim of Crime Help Line	(800) 394-2255
National Center on Elder Abuse Hotline	(800) 677-1116
National Capital Poison Control Center	(800) 222-1222
DivorceCare	(800) 268-1343

Bibliography

Farrar-Rosemon, C. Joyce. *How to Be the HEAD and NOT the TAIL!: A Christian Manifesto for Making Six Figures.* Franklin, Tenn.: Providence House Publishers, 2005.

Farrar-Rosemon, C. Joyce. *Who Stole My Blanket?: 6 Easy Steps to Rebuild Your Life After an Income Loss.* Atlanta, GA., Winner At Life Publishers, 2013.

Gardner, Chris. *The Pursuit Of Happyness,* New York: Amistad, 2006.

Parrish, Lydia. *Slave Songs Of The Georgia Sea Islands.* Athens, Georgia: (A Brown Thrasher Book) The University of Georgia Press, 1992.

Sullivan, Otha Richard. *African American Women Scientists and Inventors.* (New York: Wiley, 2002), 27.

Washington, James M., ed., *A Testament Of Hope*: *The Essential Writings And Speeches Of Martin Luther King, Jr.* (New York: Harper Collins, 1991), 286.

Whalley, Paul. *Butterfly and Moth.* (New York: Dorling Kindersley, 2000), 24-25.

Wilkinson, Bruce. *The Prayer of Jabez.* (Sisters, Oregon: Multnomah Publishers, Inc., 2000), 9-10.

About the Author

C. Joyce Farrar-Rosemon, BA, SM, Ed.S., never envisioned as she sat on the inner city housing projects steps in Boston that she would become a successful businesswoman who would one day earn a six figure income and go on to become a highly acclaimed Motivational Speaker. In 1992, Joyce married and opened a real estate company in her seventh month of pregnancy with only $10.00 in the operating account. That investment subsequently blossomed into a six-figure income.

Joyce has not only survived, but has thrived after living in a dysfunctional family. She has overcome poverty, abuse, loneliness, depression, job loss, a stillbirth and two miscarriages. Joyce has gone from making six figures-- to no figures. Following the collapse of the real estate industry in 2007, Joyce experienced unemployment and worked several low paying jobs for two years. During that time, she returned to school-- and after filling out close to 400 applications, Joyce eventually landed a job as a Certified Educator at the age of 57.

Farrar-Rosemon speaks frequently to nonprofit groups, schools, colleges and churches. She has appeared in several newspapers, magazines, on radio and television, including The Geraldo at Large Show. She is now a best-selling author, Certified Educator, Radio Host of *Inspirational Voices,* and holds a bachelor's degree in psychology and elementary education and a master's in psychiatric social work from Simmons College in Boston, Massachusetts. Joyce earned her Specialist Degree in Education from Mercer University in the fall of 2012. She and her husband, Tillmon H. Rosemon Jr., live in Atlanta, Georgia. They have one son, David.

For information on how to book Joyce for speaking engagements, or Empowerment Seminars, visit www.womensempowermentseminars.com or email Joyce at joycerosemon@gmail.com.

www.ingramcontent.com/pod-product-compliance
Lightning Source LLC
LaVergne TN
LVHW010930110826
845149LV00013B/2530

* 9 7 8 0 9 8 5 6 2 6 2 2 8 *